How California Schools Work

This book is <u>not</u> about how California schools should work. Or will work. Or have worked.

Rather, it is a guide to how they work now — a practical guide, written by former reporters, that in plain language provides information that parents will find useful in working with schools and teachers and making decisions about the education of their children.

Topics covered include enrollment procedures, how school districts assign children to schools, tests, what the scores mean, curriculum and what to do when you have complaints about programs and teachers.

Also, day care, special education, homework, class sizes, magnet programs, gifted programs, tracking and ability clustering, charter schools, educational funding, busing, year-round schedules, vocational training, bilingual instruction, holidays, transfers and how the University of California influences the high-school curriculum.

Also, sports, afterschool programs, teacher credentials, tutoring, and how to help schools and teachers do their job.

And, some of the controversies over education — not to take sides. Often the questions are complex and reasonable people disagree on solutions. But to explain the arguments and identify possible choices.

About 9 percent of California's children attend private schools. This guide gives an overview of private schools and how they differ from public schools.

McCormack's Guides also publishes 11 relocation-newcomer guides to the metropolitan counties of California. See the back page for an order blank. See also our Web site, www.mccormacks.com. Or call 800-222-3602.

Don McCormack, the editor, and John VanLandingham, the lead writer and researcher, are former newspaper reporters and editors. Both have children who attended California public and private schools. In their newspaper days, both McCormack and Vanlandingham covered education and school boards.

For their research, McCormack and Vanlandingham visited schools, talked to teachers, administrators and school board members, and collected a wide variety of school policies and procedures.

We wish to thank all those who took the time to answer our questions and provide us with information.

Graphics by T. Graphics California.
Cover by Foster and Foster.
Editorial assistant: Martina Bailey.

Copyright © 2004 by McCormack's Guides, Inc.

Library of Congress Control Number: 2004090441

Indexed   ISBN 1-929365-33-0

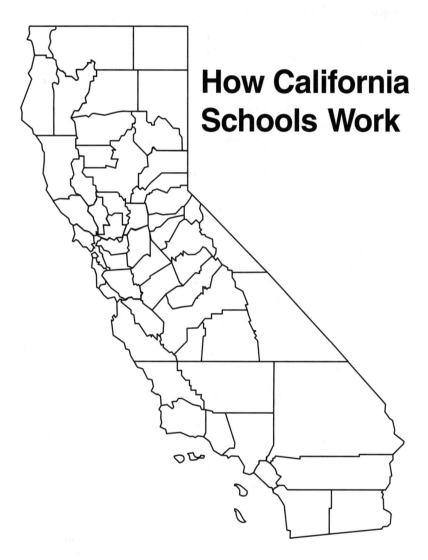

How California Schools Work

3211 Elmquist Court, Martinez, CA 94553
Phone: (800) 222-3602 & Fax: (925) 228-7223
bookinfo@mccormacks.com
www.mccormacks.com

Table of Contents

1

Choosing a School And Enrolling

- **HOW TO ENROLL**
- **ENROLLMENT EXCEPTIONS**
- **WHERE TO GET SCHOOL INFO**
- **IMMUNIZATIONS**
- **TRANSFERS**
- **PRESCHOOL ADVICE**

What's The Key Fact In Picking A Public School?

You don't pick a school. You pick an address, either by renting an apartment or buying a home or condo. The address determines which school your child attends. There are exceptions to this rule — we touch on them in this chapter — but they are few and often inconvenient.

School Boundaries

California is divided into school districts, each in control of a specific area. The districts build the schools and, typically, assign each school an attendance zone, usually the immediate neighborhood.

To find out which school your child will attend, call the local school district or school and give them your prospective address. The school personnel will identify the neighborhood school.

Many Realtors and some Web sites will have this information. But some school districts change boundaries and do not get the word out, and many districts offer choices.

School district boundaries often don't follow city boundaries. Almost all school districts established their boundaries when California had few people. When the suburbs boomed and new cities were formed, the new places grew over the school districts

Typical School District Map

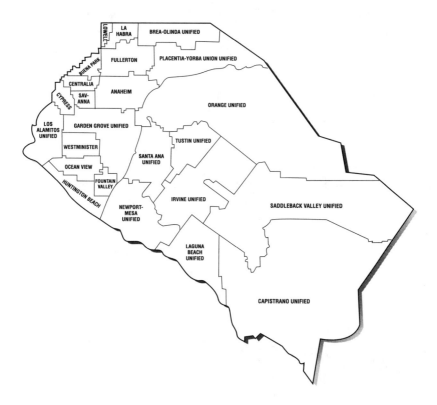

This map, somewhat simplified, shows most of the school districts for Orange County. Each district builds its own schools and assigns them attendance zones, usually the immediate neighborhood. Your address determines your school. The great majority of California students attend their neighborhood "home" school.

without realigning their borders. Many communities are served by several school districts. The City of San Jose is divided into 19 districts, a few very large, many small. It's possible for children on one street to attend one district and children just up the street or on the next block to be assigned to another district.

If there is a problem with enrolling — the school might be crowded — the school personnel will tell you straight off.

Give yourself peace of mind: Get this information directly from the school or school district.

Just say, I am moving into 1234 Main St. Which school will my children attend? District personnel will identify the school and tell you where and sometimes when to enroll.

Better Still ... Do Some Research Beforehand.

It's easy. All public schools are required to publish a School Accountability Report Card (SARC pronounced SARK). Find out the name or names of schools you are interested in and call the school and ask for its SARC. Many SARCS are posted on Web sites.

If the school person doesn't know what you are talking about — at some schools parents rarely ask for these reports — say you are interested in the report with the school scores.

California Relocation Guides

For an overview of scores and a list of schools by district, McCormack's publishes annual relocation guides with school rankings for almost all the metropolitan counties of California. See order blank at the end of this book or our Web site at www.mccormacks.com. These guides also contain SAT scores, college attendance numbers, city profiles, school-district phone numbers, crime stats, a directory of private schools and ,in most guides, directories of preschools and day-care and infant-care centers, and more.

Or go to the Web site of the California Dept. of Education, www.cde.ca.gov, and follow prompts to STAR scores. Public-school students are tested every year. The state Web site contains a lot of information about the schools.

SARCS include:

• Test scores for the school. See chapters 5 and 6 on Tests and What Scores Mean.

• Ethnic makeup of the student body.

• How many teachers are credentialed, noncredentialed or have emergency credentials. The last group includes substitutes who meet minimum qualifications of a bachelor's degree but do not have a regular teaching credential.

• Programs offered at the school.

• Class sizes.

• Information about the curriculum and school facilities and more.

A note on including ethnic data in the SARC: One law prohibits Realtors and newspapers in advertising or sales presentations from identifying homes or neighborhoods by race or ethnicity. Our society wants race, age and sexual orientation eliminated from housing choices.

At a later time, lawmakers decided that it was important to know how schools were mixing the children by ethnicity and how various ethnic groups were scoring. And so the ethnic information was placed in the SARC report. One upshot: Realtors often do not hand out the SARC reports. It might put them in violation of the housing laws.

Once you have identified schools that you like, look for homes and apartments in the attendance area.

Herculean Task

In 2003, the City of Hercules in Northern California voted to spend up to $75,000, if necessary, to verify student addresses. Hercules is a middle-class town where most of the schools score about the 50th percentile. Many schools in the nearby towns score much lower. Residents complained that the school district was allowing too many transfers into Hercules schools and not checking address or guardianship claims. Some students, one resident said, were claiming local addresses but putting down out-of-town phone numbers. The school district said it would try to do a better job.

Other Questions — Steps To Take:

• Find out the name of the connecting middle school and high school. The typical progression: kids in A Elementary move up to B Middle School, then C High School; that is, they stay together throughout their K-12 education.

• Get the school schedule and the school hours. Some schools run year-round. Hours of attendance may vary by district.

• Visit the school. See if it's clean and in good repair. If you can, talk to the principal and visit classrooms. Often, you can get a sense of the school by what's happening in the secretary's office. For example, is it noisy? Are several students lined up to see the principal? That might indicate disciplinary problems. Note: For safety reasons, all visitors must go to the school administrative office first.

• If the school has an information packet, ask for it.

• Is there busing? How much? If your child is to walk to school, check the route for safety.

• Ask if the school district has passed a renovation bond in the last 10-15 years. The great majority of public schools have passed at least one bond. If your prospective district has not, it might indicate funding problems.

Try To Identify The Unacceptable Situation

For many parents, scores are the dividing line. If a school is scoring low, they reject it outright (but these days the high price of housing is forcing many to buy into neighborhoods with low scores).

Over the last 25 years, short of money, the state has offered extra money to schools that run "year-round" schedules. See Chapter 2, Schedules.

Some parents dislike these schedules. If you have two children and one has a traditional summer vacation and starts school after Labor Day and the second has several weeks off in the fall and starts school in mid-August, your life, especially if you work or if you are a single parent, can get complicated.

Some parents might conclude, "Well no, I can't do this — it's an unacceptable situation." Shop for housing in another school district.

A few school districts, lacking financial support from their voters, may have shortened their instruction time or made other cuts that you find unacceptable. Ask about funding and crowding.

In some districts, the elementary school scores at one level, the middle school at another level and the high school at yet another level. If scores are your criteria, check this out. See Chapter 6.

At least one large district buses students out of their neighborhood schools to get social and ethnic variety. If this arrangement is unacceptable, pick a home in a town with a different setup.

Your child loves the arts. The local school has a good arts program; a school in the next county has a great arts program. You might be able to get your child into the second school. Make inquiries.

To meet the needs of its students, a school might load up on some parts of the curriculum and skimp on others. A low-scoring school might skip science and spend more time on reading and math. You might want a different program for your child.

Many schools have on-site child care, both before school and after. But some don't. You have to make the arrangements. If you have several children and one is too young for school and one is of school age, check the day care-preschool setup.

Many Parents Compromise

Scores correlate closely with community or neighborhood income. The higher the scores, the higher the income — and the higher the home price or rent. See Chapter 6 for a discussion on this topic; there are exceptions.

You may fall in love with a school and not be able to afford a home in the attendance area.

Or you can afford the home but it's old, small and cramped. For the same amount of money, you can buy a large new home in another city — with lower scores.

Or you can afford a high-scoring district and a nice home but the commute is horrible.

What do you do? You compromise. Happens all the time. This doesn't mean that you condemn your children to an inferior education. Many middle and some low-scoring schools graduate students into the top universities. But you and your children might have to work harder at academics.

Transfers

If you are dissatisfied with your child's school, you can request a transfer. Many schools will grant them. State law requires school districts to consider transfers to ease parental hardship. This might include working in one town and living in another. You transfer your child to a school near your job.

When in doubt, ask. It never hurts.

If you get nothing else from this book, hold on to this: If you have a problem, ask the school if it can help. Sometimes it won't be able to. School officials, however, don't want unhappy parents and students. If they can solve a problem without creating other problems, they will generally try to do just that. And they might have solutions that you did not think of.

Transfers Within Districts And Open Enrollment

Many districts give preference to transfer requests from children living within the home district.

Johnny attends school in the XYZ district. He would like to attend a different school within the XYZ district. Susie lives in the STUV district; she wants to transfer to the same school in the XYZ district.

Both students may be granted their requests but if space is short, the district will generally favor Johnny because he lives in the XYZ (home) district and Susie doesn't.

How to Keep Schools Open

In 2003, the Ojai school district and the adjoining Ventura district in Ventura County got into a spat over transfers. Ojai was not building affordable housing for families and was seeing its enrollments decline. The district was faced with closing schools and firing teachers — something that residents wanted to avoid. Several schools in the Ventura district but close to Ojai were scoring lower than Ojai schools. Word got out that the Ojai district welcomed transfers from the Ventura district. Parents applied to Ojai district and Ventura district objected. The parents appealed to the County Board of Education, which has final say, and the transfers were approved.

Before the start of school in the fall, districts are required by law to offer "open enrollment." In this time period, you can apply for any school in the district — space permitting. Some districts will post notices of which schools have open seats.

The rub is that space often does not permit transfers (but this could be changing. Many schools are seeing their enrollments drop.)

After "open enrollment" closes, administrators put together their plans for each school.

Late requests for transfers are discouraged or rejected because they disrupt operations.

Incidentally, the district probably will not pay for busing to the "new" school.

Transfers — No Child Left Behind

Congress recently passed a law — No Child Left Behind — that allows parents to transfer children out of low-scoring schools that fail to improve over a certain time, about two years. In 2003, this law kicked in and many parents transferred their kids out of their home schools into other schools within their home districts — but not into other districts.

How this law turns out remains to be seen. One big problem: available space at other schools. Often they don't have room for additional students.

Another problem: money. The feds are supposed to put up the money to make this work. Some money is coming but with the federal budget now in deep deficit, not as much as promised, some critics contend.

Safety, Health Or Academic Transfers

Say your child is being bullied or just not thriving in one setting and clearly a transfer would help. One district will accept the transfer with the understanding that when it has the same problem, the other district will reciprocate. Talk to the teacher or principal. Sometimes your doctor may have to write a note.

Other Situations That Encourage Or Allow Transfers

Charter schools generally can accept students from outside their immediate neighborhoods. See Chapter 7 for information about programs.

Large districts sometimes offer magnet or enriched programs designed to draw kids out of their neighborhood schools thereby breaking down segregation caused by housing costs. Or they offer arts academies at certain high schools because many students want this program.

Some high schools offer programs open to all students in the region. The Orange County High School of the Arts accepts students from throughout Orange County.

About eight of the highest-scoring high schools in the state admit students according to their scores or academic prowess.

Students having trouble are often assigned to continuation high schools that usually draw from the entire school district.

Middle-college high schools gather underperforming teenagers at community-college campuses. The theory is that college may rub off on the kids and make them better learners.

Students with serious learning disabilities may be clustered at certain schools that specialize in this type of education.

Money Transfers

The state funds local schools according to enrollment. For every student enrolled, districts receive about $5,000. (In reality, funding varies widely; many arguments).

School X has room for 100 fifth-grade students but has enrolled only 95. It fills three classes with 25 students each and the fourth class with 20. If it can add five students to its last class, it will secure more money from the state without increasing its expenses.

XYZ district has enough students to fill five schools but some of the schools have empty classrooms. If the district can fill more classrooms, its costs will rise but it would still "make" money.

Local Priorities

Several years ago, Fullerton school district in Orange County, one month into the school year, discovered that it had more students than anticipated. At this point, the district expelled kindergarten and primary students who lived outside the district — harsh but true to the district's values. It had to give priority to children who lived within the district.

When times are tough and the state is in financial trouble — like now — some districts crack down on truants. Or a district might stop checking addresses of students. (See "How to Keep Schools Open," page 12.) The more seats filled, the more money the district gets.

Why Schools Deny Transfers — Space

Although state and federal agencies give money to local schools, much of the funding, especially for construction, comes from local taxes passed by voters within the districts.

When school districts seek local approval for a funding measure, they tell voters that this money is going for your children or your neighbor's children. It's not going for the kids in the next district or the next county. Schools districts don't build extra classrooms or add extra programs for "outside" students. With rare exceptions, they don't compete for kids outside their districts.

Why Schools Deny Transfers — Money

For a student to transfer, especially between districts, he or she must often receive permission from the home school and from the transfer-in school. In some instances, the home school might not let go. The school funding formula rewards attendance.

School X has room for 100 fifth-grade students and has enrolled 100 and divided them among four classes. If it allows five students to transfer, it still has to run the classes but its funding gets cut by about $25,000.

For small districts, losing just a few students is a big deal. They may have to close a school and lay off teachers.

Why Schools Deny Transfers — Disruptions, Flexibility

District XYZ has five elementary schools, of which four score about the 50th percentile, middling, and one scores in the 90th percentile, high.

Guess which school will get many applications? School districts frequently discourage these transfers because they're disruptive and cause bad feelings. Often the kids requesting the transfers are also high-scoring. If they are allowed to transfer out of their neighborhood school into the high-scoring school, the scores will go down at the first school and rise even higher at the second, accentuating the differences between the schools and bringing more requests for transfers.

Districts try to avoid situations where one school has loads of students and others few. Say a student is shy and Miss J, one of the teachers, is especially good about drawing kids out. Or several parents complain about the classroom style of Miss K, another teacher. Or Johnny's parents specifically ask that he be placed in Miss B's class.

If a school has multiple classes at each grade level, it can accommodate many of these requests or situations. If it has only one class per grade level, then its room to maneuver is limited.

In some situations, spreading out or adjusting enrollments may lower costs. Or allow the district to run more efficiently. Or avoid disputes over teacher transfers or layoffs.

Schools may seem to be simple, one-dimensional institutions. Actually, they're complex and limited in what they can do by laws, labor contracts and social pressures.

Why Many Parents Shun Transfers

Often transfers raise havoc with your personal and work life. If your child attends the local school, you usually will make friends with other parents at that school. These parents will live in your neighborhood.

If you're late getting home from work, they can pick up your child at day care or the school and look after him or her. If you're sick, they can drive your child to school. If your child gets sick at school and has to be picked up right away, and you work 70 miles away, your neighbor might pitch in. You reciprocate for them in other ways.

If your child goes to school in another town, these arrangements become more difficult.

As the children get older, they may want to join afterschool sports or activities. Someone has to drive them to these activities and pick them up. The schools will not supply transportation. Again neighbors and school parents come in handy. If your child attends an "outside" school, you may have to look for sports and activities in that city — complications.

The children will make friends in the neighborhood and may come to resent not being able to go to school with them.

You want to make friends with the other moms and dads. You

want to get the gossip about what's really happening at the school. It's harder when you live out of district.

American parents, for good reason, are very fond of their neighborhood schools.

Unusual Situations

- **Los Angeles Unified School District.** This is the second largest in the United States. It has the money to build new schools but often has to tear down buildings in established neighborhoods and deal with irate residents. Construction has been slow and many schools have become crowded. Some schools are diverting students out of their neighborhoods to schools with space. The L.A. district runs complex and diverse programs that influence enrollment patterns and schedules. These programs include schools for high-scoring or high-ability kids. The district has some of the lowest- and the highest-scoring schools in the state. Get the enrollment information early. Also ask for the booklet on "Choices," which describes the various programs. Many of these programs have application deadlines and are limited to children already enrolled in the district. New students are assigned a home school; then they can apply for a transfer.

Transfers for Academic Reasons

High-scoring schools get more transfer requests than low-scoring. Here's a common scenario:

The schools in District X score in the 10th to 40th percentile, low to low-middle.

Just over the border or close by is the upper-income District Y which scores in the 70th to 90th percentile, top 30 percent in the state.

Rarely will parents in the high-scoring district request a transfer to schools in the low-scoring district.

As for the parents in the low-scoring district, just the opposite: many requests for transfers.

In the past, schools were under no obligation to accept these transfers but this might change with the No-Child-Left-Behind law.

- **San Francisco Unified School District.** After the courts did away with a racial integration program, this district, to promote diversity, chose to decide many placements by socioeconomic background (income, parents' education, etc.). Many students are bused out of their neighborhood schools. Some placements are decided by computer. This policy has angered many parents; it may be revised.

- **Rapidly-growing districts.** Even when land is cheap and empty and neighborhood fights can be avoided, school construction, for money and design reasons, often lags behind housing development. Some children may be reassigned out of their neighborhoods, then returned when schools are built. The closest school to your home might not be your "neighborhood" school. It might be a school assigned to another housing tract. Some districts may provide free busing based on the distance from school. Those who live, say, within a mile of the school, walk; those who live beyond a mile, get the buses.

- **Low-enrollment schools.** Every year schools are closed because enrollment has dropped. Typically, these schools are in slow-growth areas where home prices are high and beyond the reach of many young families. Ask the district if it is thinking about closing the school. Low-enrollment schools are often friendly and intimate; everyone will come to know your child's name. But these schools may have to combine grades or skimp on electives. Teacher choice will be limited.

- **First come, first served.** Some districts run fundamental or enriched schools with high or fairly high scores. Enrollment is first come, first served. Parents may camp out to get their kids into these schools. A few schools use a lottery to decide a portion of their enrollments.

- **Divorced couples have an extra choice.** Their children may be able to attend schools in dad's district or mom's. All depends on whose address is claimed for residency.

- **Overflow.** Some districts may publish an "overflow" list. It says, "Your local school is full; please make a choice from the following," and it provides a list of choices. The district may provide busing to the listed schools.

Admission Ages

To get into kindergarten, your child must turn five before Dec. 3 of the year he enters the grade. If your child's birthday falls close to this date or if she is mature for her age, check with the school. There may be wiggle room. For first grade, age 6 before Dec. 3.

When To Enroll

As soon as you can! For most children, enrollment will be simple and quick. If space is short at the school, when you apply might make a difference.

For complex districts, notably Los Angeles and San Francisco, it is especially important to enroll early and to understand the enrollment options.

What To Bring At The Time of Enrollment

In the following pages, we carry the enrollment forms from a typical district. Here is a summary of what will be requested:

• Child's birth certificate (might be waived for high school students).

• Home deed or loan-ownership papers with your name and address listed. Or current tax bill with your name and address. Or a utility bill with your name and address. Or a rental agreement with your name and address.

If a district or school gets many requests for transfers, it often will be a stickler for proof of residence. On the other hand, if it gets few requests or would like to pick up students, it might not make a fuss over addresses. Sometimes it boils down to the money. If it's not a problem, why spend money on it?

• Immunization records

• Transcripts for older children. For students transferring into upper grades, the welcoming school will ask the former school for transcripts.

For high-school students, you should have your own set of transcripts. This way the school can place the student into the appropriate classes right away (while the official transcripts are being sent).

Immunizations

You are required to show proof of immunization for polio, diphtheria, hepatitis B, tetanus, pertussis (whooping cough), measles, rubella and mumps. If the child is seven or older, you can skip mumps and whooping cough. Continuing students above the seventh grade must show proof of being immunized against hepatitis B.

Some counties might add a tuberculosis test. And often one immunization is not enough; some require booster shots. Get the full list from the school.

If your religion prohibits all or certain immunizations, you will be asked to sign a waiver acknowledging this.

Some Advice On Immunizations

Your doctor or HMO will almost always know what's required. Just ask for the school immunization battery. Or ask the school secretary to recommend a local doctor.

Some groups sponsor immunization clinics. The school often will have the information on the clinics.

Health Insurance

You can buy health insurance that will cover your children at school and home, around the clock. The insurance covers health, dental and vision and costs $4 to $9 a month per child or $27 for all the children in a family. If you can't afford this, you may be eligible for free coverage. For information, call (800) 880-5305. This insurance is called Healthy Families and is sponsored by insurance companies, teacher and school-employee unions and the California Parent-Teachers Association.

Other Pertinent Information

- **Student's medical history.** Allergies, medical problems that the school should be aware of, glasses, medications. If your child has a condition that requires special attention, you should tell the school. (Parents often are not aware of learning disabilities. Typically, these are picked up by the kindergarten or first-grade teacher, who will refer the student for tests.)

- **Doctor's Physical Exam.** Not required for entry into school or for kindergarten students. First-graders must have a physical exam before the end of the school year.
- **Special Programs.** If student was in a special or advanced program at previous school, this should be noted. It will help the school place your child in the right setting.
- **Names, addresses and phone numbers.** Mom and dad or both. Where you can be reached. Or legal guardian. Friends or relatives to contact if you are not available.
- **Ethnicity.**
- **Language.** What language is spoken at home and other questions to determine proficiency.
- **Other schooling.** You might be asked if your child attended preschool or kindergarten or language immersion classes.
- **Dental information.** Some districts ask for it.

Registration Policy

Sample from a California school district

1. A student is not registered until the school or the district assigns the student a registration date.

2. A registration date is secured when ALL required information and documents have been submitted by parents, signed and verified by the appropriate school or district personnel.

3. Parents/guardians are required by the district to provide correct and current information regarding the home address of the parent/legal guardian with whom the child resides and to report any changes in that address.

4. An address within a particular attendance area does not guarantee the registered child attendance at that elementary school. When classes, grades or schools are over-enrolled, students are moved to other schools on the basis of the home school registration date, and this may affect your student.

5. Reassignment to another school may take place after a child has begun to attend the home school.

6. Parents are responsible for transporting children to the school where they are assigned.

7. When students are not able to attend their home school because of over-enrollment at the home school, the registration date will be the determining factor of the order of recall to the home school when space permits.

8. The district may deem it necessary to further verify a child's legal residence with a home visit by school administrators who may be accompanied by a School Resource Officer from the local police department.

9. If it is determined that a child does not reside at the address claimed, parents will be required to register the child immediately at the school that does correspond with the actual address of the child.

10. Most schools allow students to apply to schools outside the attendance boundaries.

You will need to fill out a declaration of residency form and attach (be prepared to show) a current copy of at least two of the following with your name and address imprinted:

- Grant deed
- Property tax statement
- Gas and electric company statement, which will have address.
- Rental agreement
- State or federal income-tax return

Student Health and Development Questionnaire

Sample from a California school district

Questions concerning your child:
1. - Length of Pregnancy
   - Birth Weight
   - Delivery: Normal or Caesarean
   - Condition of Baby at Birth: Normal, Blue or Weak
   - Approximate Ages when student:
     - Sat alone
     - Crawled
     - Walked alone
     - Used words clearly
     - Used sentences

2. Do any of the following apply to your child?
   - Allergies: food, hay fever, seasonal, asthma?
   - Frequent ear infections
   - Hearing problem suspected
   - Known hearing loss
   - Tubes in ears
   - Speech difficulty
   - Vision problems
   - Frequent sore throats, colds, cough
   - Chicken pox
   - Chronic skin disorder
   - Convulsions or seizure
   - Diabetes
   - Bee sting reaction
   - Fainting spells

3. Are there any concerns or problems regarding your child's heart, urinary system, neurological system, bones, joints or muscles. Also, emotions or behavior?

4. Has your child had any operations, injuries or major illnesses? If so, specify the nature and approximate dates.

5. Does your child take any regular prescribed medication? What kind?

6. Is your child able to participate in a regular physical education program? If no, why?

7. If your child is entering kindergarten, has he/she attended a nursery or preschool program?

Parent Assessment of Kindergarten Readiness
Sample from a California school district

• Does your child or can your child:
- state his/her complete name?
- recite home address?
- recite home telephone number?
- know full name of parent/guardian?
- state his/her birth date?

• How often is your child read to by an adult: daily, two times a week or less than once a week?

• Is your child's speech easily understood by:
- you?
- other adult family members?
- peers?

• Indicate what preschool experiences your child has had by giving name(s) of school(s), dates of attendance and teachers' names.

• What other experiences has your child had with other groups of children, for example, play groups, sports, dance?

• How would you characterize your child's ability to associate with groups of children and deal with new situations?

• What special services, if any, does your child now receive; for example, speech, occupational or physical therapy, counseling?

Delayed or conditional admissions
You want to enroll your child in a certain school (not your home school) but the principal can't say yes or no until she sees what the regular enrollment brings.

She might say, we can admit your child but if we get too many "home" students, she will have to leave.

Or enroll your child in the home school and if we have space in October (when they have a count of new students) we will admit her.

Your choice. Some parents don't want to place the child in one school then uproot her a month later for another school.

Preschool Report of Kindergarten Readiness
Sample from a California school district

This form is filled out by the preschool your child attended.

1. How long has the child been enrolled at preschool?

2. What do you (the preschool) use to assess school readiness?

3. What special services, if any, does the child receive? For example, speech, counseling?

4. Does your program provide:
   - regular preschool program?
   - daily child care; no formalized preschool program?
   - preschool and day care combined?

5. Observations
   - right- or left-handed?
   - grasps pencil with fist or fingers?
   - do hearing and vision appear to be normal?

6. Behavior/Social Interaction
   Does the child:
   - play alone successfully?
   - play with groups successfully?
   - stay on task as appropriate to age level?

7. Skills and Abilities
   Can the child:
   - Verbally give his/her first name, full name, age, address and birth date?
   - Recognize and identify colors?
   - Recognize and name a circle, square, triangle and rectangle?
   - Copy a straight line, a circle, a cross, a square and a triangle?
   - Hop on one foot?
   - Stand on one foot momentarily? For five seconds?
   - Count to 10?
   - Listen to, remember and follow a one-step direction? Two-step direction?
   - Print his/her first name?
   - Is the child's speech understandable? Does he/she speak in complete sentences?

Home Language Questions

Sample from a California school district

The California Education Code requires schools to determine the language(s) spoken at home by each child. If you indicate that your student speaks a language other than English, the student's English fluency will be assessed.

You will need to give your student's date and place of birth. If the child was not born in the United States, when did he/she enter the country? When did he/she enter California?

1. Which language did your child learn when he/she first began to talk?

2. What language does your child most frequently use at home?

3. What language do you use most frequently to speak to your child?

4. Name the language most often spoken by the adults at home.

5. If a language other than English is indicated in answers to any of the questions above, does your child understand this language?

6. Can the child speak, read or write this language?

7. How many years did the child spend in schools outside of the United States?

8. When was the child first enrolled in a U.S. school? How many years has he/she attended school in the United States?

9. Number of years in English learner classes?

10. Is your child of American-Indian ancestry? If so, what tribe?

How to Choose a Preschool

For most kids, preschool and day care are woven together. Parents are working, someone has to take care of the kids, enter the preschool, the day-care center.

Here is some advice offered by a person who runs a preschool and day-care center.

- **Ask about age restrictions.** Many centers and family-care providers will not take care of children under age 2 or not toilet trained.

- **Give the center or home a visual check.** Is it clean? In good condition or in need of repairs? Is there a plan for repairs when needed?

- **Find out if the person in charge is the owner or a hired manager.** Nothing wrong with the latter but you should know who is setting policy and who has the final say on matters.

- **Ask about the qualifications of the people who will be working directly with your child.** How long have they worked in day care? Training? Education? Many community colleges offer training in early childhood and afterschool care.

- **Find out if the place is simply doing day-care or has a preschool program,** that is, a program to help get your kid ready for school.

- **What philosophy or approach does the center use?** The Piaget approach believes children move through three stages and by exploring, the child will naturally move through them. The job of the teacher is to provide activities appropriate to the right stage. For example, from age 2-7, many children master drawing and language; from 7-11, they begin to think logically. For the younger child, art and sorting and language games would be appropriate; multiplication would not.

  Montessori believes that, if given the right materials and placed in the right setting, children will learn pretty much by themselves through trial and error. Montessorians employ specific toys for teaching.

  Traditional approaches emphasize structure and repetition.

These descriptions are oversimplified and do not do justice to these approaches or others. Our only purpose here is to point out that day-care providers vary in methods and thinking, and in choosing a center, you also choose a distinct philosophy of education.

- **For family day-care providers.** Some set up a small preschool setting in the home. Often your child will be welcomed into the family as an extended member. Is this what you want?
- **Discipline.** Johnny throws a snit. How is it handled? Does the provider have a method or a plan? Do you agree with it?
- **Tuition.** How much? When is it due? Penalty for picking up child late? Penalty for paying late?
- **Hours of operation.** If you have to be on the road at 5:30 a.m. and the day-care center doesn't open until 6, you may have to look elsewhere or make different arrangements. Some centers limit their hours of operation, e.g., 10 hours.
- **Holidays.** For family providers, when will the family take a vacation or not be available? For the centers, winter breaks? Summer vacations?
- **Communication.** Ask how you will be kept informed about progress and problems. Regular meetings? Notes? Calls? News-letters?
- **Classes-Tips for parents.** Opportunities to socialize with other parents? Activities for the whole family?
- **Field trips and classes.** Outside activities. Your son and daughter play soccer, an activity outside the day-care center. How will they get to practice? What's offered on site? Gymnastics? Dance?
- **Siestas.** How much sleep will the children get? When do they nap? Does this fit in with your child's schedule?
- **Activities.** What are they? How much time on them? Goals?
- **Diapers, bottles, cribs, formula, extra clothes.** Who supplies what?
- **Food, lunches.** What does the center serve? What snacks are available?

Remember, day-care centers and preschools are in business. The people who staff and manage these facilities and homes may have the best intentions toward the children but if they can't make a profit or meet payrolls, they will fail or be unable to provide quality care. Even "nonprofits" must be run in a businesslike way or they won't survive.

Some centers may offer a rich array of services but for fees beyond your budget. You have to decide the trade-offs.

McCormack's publishes relocation-newcomer guides for the metropolitan counties of California. Almost all our guides have directories of day-care and infant-care centers, broken out by city. See www.mccormacks.com or order blank at end of book.

Or check the Yellow Pages.

Just about every county will have a child-care agency with a list of preschools and day-care centers.

Enrollment Dropping

Between 1990 and 2001, births in California dropped from 611,666 a year to 527,371, a difference of 84,295 babies or 14 percent. The baby-boom generation, now well into its 40s and 50s, is no longer producing babies and families are having fewer children, demographers note.

In 2002, California closed 57 public schools, most of them located in farmlands and older suburbs. Some districts, paticularly those in the new inland suburbs, are still growing. But where home prices are high and new construction is sparse, schools are seeing the enrollments decrease, especially in the lower grades.

The Los Angeles district, biggest in the state, is adding students — about 10,000 a year but most of them are middle-schoolers and high-school students. In the elementary grades, the district, between 1995 and 2002, lost about 4,300 students. Schools are treasured institutions; many towns hate to close them. Rather than close schools, many districts have cut or combined classes and some are looking at redrawing attendance boundaries to move students out of crowded schools into schools with space.

This situation might make it easier to win a transfer to a high-scoring school. Many of these schools are located in old towns with high prices — often the places losing enrollment.

2

Who's In Charge?

- • OVERVIEW OF STATE SETUP
- • CALIFORNIA DEPT. OF EDUCATION
- • HOW SCHOOLS ARE ORGANIZED.
- • SCHOOL BOARDS, SUPERINTENDENTS, PRINCIPALS
- • OTHER PLAYERS

This book is about the kindergarten-through-grade-12 (K-12) system, public and private. But to understand the K-12 system, it's helpful to look at the systems and players that tie into it.

Typical Progression — College Bound

- • **Preschool,** generally ages 3 and 4.
- • **Elementary School,** usually kindergarten through fifth or sixth grade.
- • **Middle school,** grades five to eight, or junior high, grades seven and eight.
- • **High School,** grades 9-12.
- • **College.** Many students attend out-of-state or private colleges but the great majority attend public colleges and universities within the state. Although governed separately, the public colleges and universities greatly influence instruction at the K-12 schools.

Preschool (And Day Care)

Except for Head-Start programs for low-income children, just about all preschools are privately run and many of the Head-Start schools are managed by private firms or community service groups, such as the YMCA, under contract with a public agency.

Many preschools function as day-care centers and as schools and it's important to know the difference. A day-care center may limit itself just to keeping the kids busy, fed and out of harm and mischief.

A preschool is supposed get the kids academically and socially ready for kindergarten or the first grade. Some of these schools follow distinct learning philosophies, for example, Montessori or Carden. See end of Chapter 1 for advice on choosing a preschool. In recent years, educators have elevated the importance of pre-schools, especially Head Start, because many children are entering school unprepared for academics.

Regarding day care for school-age children, most elementary schools include a center that offers before-and-after child care, at parents' expense. Some cities subsidize day care, the amount depending on the parents' income.

Kindergarten Through 12 (K-12) System

About 91 percent of students attend public school. This chapter covers the public sector; Chapter 15, private schools. Although their curriculums differ, much of what is taught in the public schools is also taught in the private simply because the students need to master the same knowledge: math, geometry, science, etc. Also because both public and private schools, in their college-prep classes, follow the dictates of the University of California.

Community Colleges

Enrollment about 1.7 million, full- and part-time, in an academic year. California has 108 community colleges scattered around the state. Just about every county will have one or will have a branch campus. No academic admission requirements but when confronted with classwork, homework and grades, many students drop out.

Community colleges train people in job skills and for careers, such as nursing, child care, office-secretarial, culinary-restaurant.

They teach the academic curriculum for lower-division university work (freshman, sophomore). Many "university" students attend community colleges for the first two years because they charge little and are within short drives (the students can live at home). The students then transfer as juniors to a California State University or a University of California.

Some high-school students take classes at community colleges to fill academic requirements.

Community colleges boast that their instructors do a better job than many university professors. The former are hired for their academic knowledge (many these days have Ph.Ds) and their teaching ability. Many start out as teachers in the K-12 schools. University professors are hired for their academic knowledge and for their research prowess; teaching ability may be secondary.

Community colleges are supposed to be community oriented. Their governing boards are elected locally. In designing their curriculums, these colleges will confer with local industries or firms to see what skills are in demand. They also consult the local high schools and try to mesh (or "articulate") their programs so students can move easily from high school to college.

Many community colleges offer summer enrichment classes for adolescents and teens— a cheap way to keep the kids interested in academics.

California State Universities

Also called CSU's or Cal States, for example, Cal State Hayward, Long Beach State, San Diego State. Enrollment about 407,000, including post-grads. Twenty-three campuses, almost all of them in metropolitan areas and many branch campuses. Instruction covers four years of college and master's degree or equivalent (such as teacher's certificate.) Two campuses specialize in the sciences: Cal State Pomona and San Luis Obispo.

Admission requirements: top one-third of high-school class and completion of the prep curriculum (see chapter on programs).

Cal State professors, almost all Ph.Ds, are hired for their academic knowledge and accomplishments, and for their teaching skills. Cal States, with few exceptions, can't offer the Ph.D. They are not research institutions.

All or almost all Cal States have dorms and attract students from around the state and indeed from around the nation and the world. In the big cities, Cal States function as commuter universities, popular with young students and mature adults returning to school to pick up a belated bachelor's or master's. Cal States offer extension classes — non-degree or certificate classes.

Cal States are managed by professional educators appointed by a state board. No local elections. The state board is appointed by the governor with the approval of the state Senate.

University Of California

Nine campuses, including one (San Francisco) that specializes in medicine and has almost no undergrads. About 135,000 undergrads and 42,000 grads. Offers bachelor's, master's and doctorates. UCs are also research institutions. Several UCs have Nobel winners. Some UCs are ranked among the top universities in the world.

Admission requirements, top 12.5 percent of class and perhaps another half-percent admitted under discretionary rules that seemingly are always under argument. Very competitive.

Commonly called UC this or that, as in, to name the campuses, UC Berkeley (also known as Cal), UC Davis, UCLA, UC Riverside, UC San Diego, UC Santa Barbara, UC Santa Cruz. Another UC is to open in 2005 near Merced in Central California.

Great influence on the K-12 system, particularly the high schools. To gain admission to a UC or a Cal State, a high-school student must take courses approved by the UC system.

Californians believe that if the UCs are to become and remain first class they must be free to set and enforce their own standards. The big exception: Affirmative Action (admission based on ethnicity) which voters shot down at the polls. But even with this rejection, the UCs have cobbled together standards and programs that allow the admission of a diverse group. The arguments, however, rage on.

To get into a UC generally means that you can get into the other top universities in the United States. Classes have sprung up on how to win admission to a UC and people have gone into business as UC admission gurus.

In the nuances of California life, many parents and people believe that a UC degree opens doors to more money and prestige, that UC alumni help other alumni to get the better jobs and so on. Several years ago, the L.A. Times let drop that in that part of the world it helped to a have a degree from UCLA (and from the University of Southern California). In the San Francisco area, the Berkeley (and Stanford) parchment is sometimes accorded the kowtow, especially in winning a good job after graduation.

The UC system is governed by a board of trustees appointed for the most part by the governor. Much of the power lies with the faculty. Big-time sports, especially basketball and football.

The UCs also run popular extension classes open to the public.

Private Universities

Some are world famous. Stanford, California Institute of Technology, University of Southern California, Occidental, Pepperdine. Some, particularly the Catholic institutions, enjoy excellent reputations as small colleges — Loyola Marymount, St. Mary's, University of San Diego, Santa Clara, University of San Francisco.

The private universities do not directly influence instruction at the K-12 schools but through their admission policies, practices and political and intellectual weight, they help shape educational policy.

Schools by the Numbers

•*The average cost of a hardcover textbook in 2002 was $18.78.*

•*About 675,000 students are enrolled in special education programs.*

•*About 88% of the state's teachers are credentialed.*

•*About 3% are interns and about 8% teach under an emergency (temporary) credential.*

•*For every 5.3 students, there is one computer (2002 figures).*

• *About 1.6 million K-12 students or 25% of the total state enrollment are classified as English learners, immigrants with limited command of English.*

•*About 2.5 million students speak a language other than English in their homes.*

•*The top five foreign language groups are Spanish, 84%, Vietnamese, 2%, Hmong, 2%, Cantonese, 2%, Filipino or Tagalog, 1%.*

•*About 929,000 people are enrolled in adult education. The most popular classes are English as a Second Language, 401,502 students, high school GED, 143,989 students and vocational education, 138,804 students.*

•*Between 2003 and 2008, the state expects enrollment in the K-6 grades to drop by 33,000 students and in grades 7-8, by 9,000 students. The high schools are expected to add 209,000 students.*

Source: Fact Book 2004, California Dept. of Education

The K-12 Public System

Overview

This system divides into decisions at three levels:
• State and federal
• School boards and school superintendents
• Principals and teachers.

Each level has its own powers and duties but they are supposed to work together for the good of students.

California Department of Education

The department of education is responsible for:

• Choosing the curriculum and deciding, in a large way, what will be taught. It also sets curriculum standards (what the children should learn in each grade).

• Adopting and enforcing regulations for all schools. Not all regulations; some are left to the schools themselves.

• Choosing textbooks or choosing a pool of texts that the schools can pick from. These texts often are aligned to the state curriculum. At the local level, a committee of administrators and teachers often will review the texts and make recommendations to the school board. Before texts are "adopted," they are made available for public scrutiny.

• Drawing up and managing the education budget (but the governor and the Legislature decide the amount in the budget).

• Deciding disputes over district boundaries or district reorganizations.

• Deciding what tests will be used and what graduation requirements will be required. California is supposed to start using an exit exam in 2006 for seniors — no pass, no diploma.

• Allocating federal funds to schools and districts.

• Intervening when districts blow their budgets or get into mischief. In bankruptcies, the department will often assign an administrator to make financial decisions.

• Running a few schools, notably for the deaf and blind.

• Doing research on teaching methods and programs.

K-12 Schools — Overview

School Districts

Unified School Districts (Grades K-12)	327
Elementary Districts (K-6 or K-8)	566
High-school Districts, (Gr. 9-12)	92

A unified school district covers all the grade levels but breaks them into divisions of elementary, middle or junior and high school. All are controlled by one school board and one superintendent. Most students attend schools in unified school districts. Common abbreviation: USD as in Los Angeles USD.

An elementary district covers only the elementary years and advances its students into a high-school district. The elementary district will have its own board, superintendent and staff. Most elementary districts are small.

High-school Districts. A few take in middle schools and junior highs, most are grades 9-12. Each has its own board, superintendent and staff. High-school districts give admission preference to their affiliated elementary districts. Example: in Los Angeles County, the students of the elementary districts of Castaic, Newhall, Saugus and Sulphur Springs move up to the William Hart High School District.

County Offices of Education. Every county has one, run by an elected board and an elected superintendent. These agencies provide schooling at detention facilities and help educate the disabled. They also run job training programs and monitor the budgets of the regular districts.

Public School Enrollment

K-8	4,374,967
Grades 9-12	1,807,054
Others	63,382
Total	6,244,403

Private School Enrollment

Total	609,483*

California Dept. of Education, Fact Book 2004. Data from 2002-2003 school year. Private school figure an estimate; does not include schools enrolling fewer than six students.

K-12 Schools — Overview

California has 7,668 regular public schools. It has 1,419 schools that the education department identifies as "alternative," "continuation," or some other category. We list the major groups below. Keep in mind, however, that many of the regular schools run special programs. We explain many of these programs and charter schools in Chapter 6.

Elementary Schools (K-5 or K-8)	5,456
Middle Schools (6,7,8)	1,183
Junior High Schools (7 and 8)	23
High Schools (9-12)	1,006
Continuation High Schools	522
Community Day Schools	305
Special Education Schools	123
K-12 schools	93

Class Sizes

State policies financially reward and in other ways encourage schools to limit enrollment in grades kindergarten through three to 20 students per class. These policies were installed in 1990s when the California economy was booming. With hard times, some schools districts want to bump up the class sizes. As for the other grades, many districts try to restrict classes to no more than 29 or 30 students. The average class size for all grades is 26 students (Fact Book 2004).

School Sizes

The Los Angeles District operates the most schools in the state and the most with the highest enrollments — at least seven high schools with more than 4,000 students. The state champ, from the L.A. district, Belmont High, a year-round school with about 5,000 students.

The largest school in Northern California is James Logan High in Union City, about 4,300 students.

Outside of the L.A. District and James Logan High, enrollments at high schools drop sharply and rarely get above 3,000 students. (School year 2002-2003).

Federal Government

The feds set many of the rules and provide a good deal of funding, about $7 billion, for programs. In recent years, the feds passed what is known as No Child Left Behind, legislation that affects how students are tested and how parents can deal with low-scoring schools. The No-Child laws also encourage better training for teachers. No-Child has its critics.

Normally, the federal rules are enforced by the California Dept. of Education, which also passes on the funds to the schools.

School Boards

California has 1,056 school districts and almost every one has a board and superintendent.

School boards, usually five members, are directly elected by voters within the local district. Almost invariably, they are citizen representatives: business people, civic leaders, parent activists, members of the service clubs (Rotary, Lions, etc.), and teachers not affiliated with the local schools (they may be retired or work in other districts).

School boards set budgets, hire and fire the superintendent, decide grievances, set some policy (much is decided at the state level and handed down) and in an informal way sound out community opinion on how the schools are run. When bonds are to be passed, board members will often pitch them to the public. School boards decide if a school is to be closed and determine school attendance boundaries.

Many board members earn a small salary, about $400 a month, and qualify for benefits but they are not considered part of the school staff. They are not expected to get involved in the day-to-day operations of the district. In fact, they are discouraged from doing so.

School boards convene once or twice a month in meetings open to the public. With the notable exception of litigation strategy and personnel matters, their deliberations are supposed to be made at public meetings. All votes must be conducted publicly. Often a board will meet in a legally sanctioned closed session, deliberate and then come out and vote on a motion.

School boards, with few exceptions, are separate from city halls. But over the last two decades, cities and school districts have begun to work together on recreational projects. In these arrangements, a city might partially fund a school swimming pool or gym on condition that it be open to the public in the evening or on weekends. Or the city will locate a park next to the school.

Some cities are served by multiple school districts.

State law defines the powers of the Department of Education and states, in effect, that whatever powers the state does not claim belong to the school boards. This implies that school boards have a great deal of power. Well, they have power but many a school board complains that the state takes too much on itself and leaves too little to local discretion.

Superintendents

Hired by school boards, superintendents are professional educators. Almost all started as teachers and worked up the administrative ladder. The great majority have doctorates in education.

In theory, the school board sets policy; the superintendent executes it and runs the day-to-day operations of the district. Inevitably, superintendents set or greatly influence policy because they usually know more about schools and education than the board members.

Although the school board has the last word on hiring and firing, superintendents are responsible for these duties. Typically, the board just ratifies the superintendent's choices. (The superintendent frequently asks teacher-parent committees to review teacher applications and make recommendations.)

The superintendent provides information on decisions the board has to make and often recommends a course of action. The superintendent — most important — is in charge of the budget and recommends financial actions to the board.

A few school districts are run top down; the superintendent controls all and dictates all. This style has its admirers but many districts embrace a more collegiate way of governing. Often thorny questions are massaged and amended until consensus is reached. If a superintendent is clever — many are — he or she will have a sense of what the board or the community will tolerate and how to move the board in a certain direction. With few exceptions, superintendents are gradualists. *(Continued on page 42)*

Muddling Along

The California Department of Education is awkwardly structured and this causes political fights and mix-ups.

On the one hand, the department of education is run by the California Board of Education, 11 members, almost all of them appointed by the governor with the approval of 2/3 of the state Senate.

This is a traditional and common setup in many states. The governor is responsible for the budget. Schools are the biggest item in the budget so it's only natural for the schools to be run as an administrative branch of the governor's office.

In this arrangement, the governing board typically sets policy and its administrative officer carries it out.

California does it differently.

Superintendent of Public Instruction

It directly elects a state Superintendent of Public Instruction, responsible not to the governor or the board of education but to voters. The superintendent runs the daily operations of the department of education and serves on important boards, such as the Regents of the University of California. He also serves as the executive officer of the board of education.

The post is held by Jack O'Connell, a former teacher and state legislator.

State Secretary for Public Education

For a governor to let another elected official run with education, influence budgets and control policy — hard to tolerate. So the governor appoints his own education boss, the State Secretary for Public Education, whose powers derive from the governor's control over the state budget and his appointments to the state board of education. The secretary is a shadowy figure, politically important, but lacking staff and bureaucratic powers, not involved in the day-to-day operations of the Department of Education or the schools.

The post is held by Richard Riordan, former mayor of Los Angeles.

Who's Really in Charge?

It's a muddle. Superintendent O'Connell would seem to be more important than Secretary Riordan because the secretary lacks staff and bureaucratic powers and is not involved in the day-to-day operations of the department or the schools. On the other hand, the secretary speaks for the governor and often influences policy through the board of education.

There is a political overlay to this. The superintendent's position is nonpartisan but almost everyone who holds the post has climbed to public prominence as an elected Democrat or Republican.

When the superintendent and the governor are of the same party, relations are sometimes rocky but they try to get along.

When they are from different parties, things get dicier. Riordan and his boss, Governor Arnold Schwarzenegger, are Republicans, O'Connell is a Democrat.

In the past, California educational politics have gotten downright nasty but forces are always at work to tone down disputes.

The public and parents and many teachers frown on politicians who grandstand on education. The politicians know this and tiptoe around educational questions. The same for policies. If a policy is out of the mainstream, if it's controversial and doesn't prove itself in a short time, the public and parents often withdraw their support or force major changes. Some liberals deplore the public's response, especially on such matters as Affirmative Action and bilingual education. Conservatives also have their complaints.

On many questions, California welcomes change and experimentation — as the charter schools testify. It's a mixed bag.

A committee has been appointed to review the entire state educational structure.

This committee is expected to recommend giving the governor's office more power over operations and straightening out the chain of command.

(Continued from page 39)
The district's other administrators — finance, human resources, curriculum, building, maintenance, etc. — report to the superintendent. Large districts have their own lawyers; small and medium districts keep lawyers on retainer and use as needed.

Principals also report to the superintendents and often superintendents are judged by the quality of the principals.

Principals

The principal manages the school, assigns and evaluates teachers and personnel, oversees instruction and training and helps teachers meet goals.

If parents have a complaint, often the principal will meet with them. The principal is responsible for discipline.

If something is not working, the principal is expected to fix it. Not all the time. If money is not available to fix the roof, the principal will be not found up top hammering in shingles. Principals work within the confines of a budget and must understand budgeting.

A principal may be found on yard duty and supervising the lunch room or doing whatever is necessary to keep things running. Large schools often have one or several vice principals. At many schools, the principal's secretary handles many of the smaller problems and some argue, humorously, that the secretaries really run the schools.

Principals are former teachers; many have postgraduate training. They are expected to know and comply with the rules and regulations and to be socially astute and mindful of unwritten rules, which often means consulting with the teachers on optional policy matters.

Principals decide who is to be hired and whether a probationary teacher is to be granted tenure or let go. Principals report to the superintendent. Under the "No-Child" and state regulations, principals may be removed if schools fall short of state goals. But removed may mean transferred to another administrative job or back to the classroom.

Teachers

Because they are very important, we have devoted a chapter to teachers. See Chapter 3.

Other Players

State Legislature

It passes many laws affecting education. Common scenario: One of the lobbying groups approaches a legislator and sells her or him on a program or policy change. The change is put into a bill, which is reviewed by legislative committees.

If passed by both houses, it is sent to the governor for approval. If approved, it becomes part of the state educational code. Critics charge that the code has become so complex and contradictory that it impedes rather than helps the schools. A recent development is charter schools; they are allowed to ignore many code provisions.

Unions

Almost all the key groups in education have unions, including the administrators and the janitors. The most important are the teacher unions: the California Teachers Association, 330,000 members and the California Federation of Teachers, 100,000.

The teacher unions are among the strongest backers of the Democrats. Often when unions want policy changes, they work through Sacramento and the state Legislature. Many of their proposals are intended to boost the pay and protect the jobs of its members (what unions are supposed to do). The union also fights ideas it dislikes. Historically, these have included merit pay, vouchers and charter schools (which may employ nonunion teachers). At the district level, union representatives monitor policies and negotiate contracts for their members.

Public

California allows its citizens to change state law through the ballot, bypassing the Legislature and the governor. Proponents of a measure must gather a certain amount of signatures to place the issue before voters, then it is decided at the polls. Winning initiatives have forced major changes in public education. They include Prop. 13, which radically changed how schools are funded, and measures that restricted bilingual education and forbade university officials from using ethnic data in admitting students. In reaction, new funding measures were introduced and new ways were found to deal with ethnic admissions and bilingual education. These are running battles in the California cultural-financial wars.

Business Groups

Not as well organized as unions but still influential. Business leaders are often appointed to key education committees.

Ethnic And Religious Groups

Ethnic groups lobby for programs that might help their members, for example, language instruction, and review text books to make sure, among other things, diversity is noted and applauded. Religious groups might review the wording of textbooks and make recommendations to textbook publishers or committees. Occasionally a few districts get embroiled in disputes over sex education and religious strictures.

Textbook writers, mindful of criticism, tread warily in the realm of religion and ethnic politics but California is quite secular.

Parent Groups

Parent-Teacher-Associations (PTA) are very important at many schools, especially for fund-raising. Many schools are underfunded and find it impossible to raise taxes (which often require two-thirds vote of residents). Any money raised through taxes often must be spent through the school board. Funds raised through parent and community groups, however, can be spent where the parents decide. Some schools raise hundreds of thousands for academics and electives, such as band.

In many communities, parents volunteer in the schools and come to know the teachers and principals. If you want the gossip and the opinions of who's a good teacher or bad, these parents, discreetly, will let you know. Parents also are the driving force behind certain programs. To mention just two — gifted (high-achieving) programs and special education.

School Site Councils

Various schools have a site council, an advisory group of parents, teachers and students organized to work with the principal and other administrators on curriculum, funding and policy issues.

Miscellaneous

When Districts Drop The Ball

Occasionally districts run up a deficit by overspending and are forced to apply to the state for a loan to bail them out. When that happens the state steps in to run the district, making decisions normally made by the local board. Often this results in improved operations. Sometimes a district, looking at a pending deficit, will invite the county superintendent of schools to assume fiscal oversight. In each circumstance, the local district is surrendering some or all of its authority to the state or county. One Southern California district was in such administrative disarray, the state took over the entire district.

Sometimes, however, state oversight is not so welcome. In 2003, West Contra Costa district parents hooted and booed a state administrator when he said the state was concerned about quality education as well as balancing the budget.

Local districts are at the mercy of the state budget which often is approved long after theirs.

Libraries

Local school boards must provide library services, either in the form of school libraries or by contracting with another public agency. Despite greater emphasis on school libraries in recent years, the state acknowledges they are still lagging.

Approximately 98 percent of the state's schools have some place designated as a library but the staffing of these facilities ranges from exemplary to substandard, according to the state department of education.

The current ratio of library books per student (grades K-12) is 13, up from 10 in 1986. The national recommendation is 16 to 25 depending on the size and level of the school.

3

Teachers, Counselors
& Others

- **COUNSELORS**
- **CONTRACTS AND SALARIES**
- **COMPLAINTS**

- **CREDENTIALS**
- **UNIONS**
- **TENURE AND FIRING**

Often beloved as individuals but sometimes criticized as a group, teachers are the backbone of the schools. They educate the children.

California schools employ about 310,000 teachers in grades kindergarten through 12.

Although more men are going into teaching, the profession is dominated by women. They make up 72 percent of the California teaching corps.

California teachers are the highest paid or among the highest paid in the nation but salaries remain a touchy issue because California is one of the most expensive states in the United States. Indeed, many teachers cannot afford to live in the communities in which they teach. Salaries average $34,000 (beginning teachers) to $74,000 a year, according to a 2001-2002 survey.

How To Become A Teacher

Teachers must be college graduates. With exceptions that are supposed to get fewer, teachers must secure a teaching credential (a license to teach) at an accredited college or university. They then apply for a job and serve a probation of usually three years (sometimes two). At the end, the teacher is either dismissed or hired and given tenure (job security).

The Teaching Credential

Credential requirements are changing. The following will give you some idea of the basic requirements. The credential divides as follows:

- **Professional Clear.** At least a bachelor's degree. Must pass a test called the CBEST (proficiency in reading, writing and math) and then secure a teaching degree or credential — about 1.5 years — from an accredited college or university. Must take 150 hours of "professional development" classes every five years.

- **Internship.** Bachelor's degree. Pass CBEST. Must be taking classes and pursuing a full credential.

- **Emergency.** Bachelor's degree. Pass the CBEST. Does not require enrollment in or completion of a teaching program. Has limits designed to prevent schools from hiring the emergency credentialed for a long time. Many substitute teachers work under the emergency credential.

Credential Types

Upon applying to teacher programs, applicants are asked to decide whether they want to teach in the elementary grades or the secondary (middle, junior high and high).

If elementary, applicants usually pursue a multiple-subject credential that includes classes in math, reading, science and social studies. These teachers are required to know a fair amount about many subjects.

If secondary, applicants pursue a single-subject credential. These teachers are required to know a lot about one subject: math or literature or science, etc. The course work strengthens their knowledge about a specific subject. Applicants steeped in the knowledge of their fields — an extreme example: a retired pharmacist who wants to teach chemistry — can skip the classes by passing a test.

Variations include a multiple-subject that requires Spanish proficiency and offers training in teaching to different cultures, and a multiple-subject with training in educating disabled students.

All candidates are coached on how to teach and how to run a classroom and they practice, under the eye of a supervisor, in actual classrooms.

For a full-time candidate, the course work can be covered in 4 to 7 quarters. Many candidates take about 1.5 years to secure a certificate.

Public and private universities offer the teaching credential. Some of the programs are designed for working adults who attend classes on evenings and weekends.

Getting Hired And Starting Off

Many schools use committees to hire teachers. A committee might include a teacher, a parent representative, the principal, maybe someone from the personnel office.

A large school district might hold a recruiting fair and do some screening before passing applicants to the next stage.

Once hired and depending on funds available, the beginning teacher is often coupled with a veteran teacher who offers advice and possibly sits in on some classes. The beginner is given evaluations and is expected to correct shortcomings.

At the end of two years or before the completion of the third year, the principal, usually, decides whether to hire or discharge the teacher. In these years, the teacher has just about zero job protection.

Tenured

Once tenured, the teacher comes under the protection of civil-service laws and the union contract. The union contract is negotiated by collective bargaining: Whatever contract the union and the school district agree upon sets the salary and working conditions and grievance procedures for all teachers (even those not in the union). This combination of civil service and union contract gives teachers, compared to other occupations, a high degree of job security but not 100 percent security. If a school runs short of money or out of students, teachers can be laid off. They can also be fired for:

- Immoral conduct
- Unprofessional conduct
- Unsatisfactory performance
- Dishonesty
- Incompetence
- Drug addiction

- Failure or refusal to perform normal and reasonable duties
- Felony or misdemeanor conviction involving moral turpitude
- Fraud in securing appointment
- Drunkenness on duty

Teacher Contract

The teacher contract, which usually includes counselors and teaching specialists, spells out in detail — often 40 plus pages — rights and duties. These contracts run for specified terms, usually three years, with openers allowed for salaries. A typical contract might cover:

- District rights
- Union rights
- Payroll deductions
- Work year and work day
- Grievances
- Leaves
- Evaluations
- Wages
- Health, vision, dental benefits for active and retired personnel
- Employee travel
- Transfers
- Class size
- Training for teachers with disabled students in their classes
- Health and safety conditions
- Peer assistance and review program
- Personal and academic freedom

Salaries And Seniority

Teachers are paid according to salary scale. See sample in this chapter. The longer the years of service, the higher the salary. If a teacher returns to school and picks up additional credits, her salary will be raised by $2,000 to $4,000 year. There's a small reward, about $1,000, for securing a master's or doctorate.

A few teachers are pursuing national certification, a much higher standard.

Teacher Unions

Most of California's nearly 310,000 public school teachers are represented by either the California Teachers' Association (CTA) or the California Federation of Teachers (CFT). While there are philosophical and political differences between the two, both work toward better working conditions and pay for their members.

The CTA represents more than 330,000 education workers in the state's schools, colleges and universities. Founded in 1863, it is the California affiliate of the National Education Association. The CFT, founded in 1919 as an affiliate of the American Federation of Teachers, represents more than 100,000 education workers from Head Start to the state's universities.

Problems And Advice — Overview

Although much has changed in California education over the last 10 years — the basic curriculum, tests, report cards — the ways parents interact with schools and teachers and the advice given on this subject has changed little if at all. But there are some new tactics.

The official advice: keep in touch with your child's teacher, help where you can, make sure the homework gets done, start the kid off with a good breakfast, support school activities, show up at Back-to-School-Night and Open House. All good stuff. In fact, if you do all this, the chances of your child receiving a good education will increase dramatically.

The unofficial advice, often dispensed in chats with other parents and with friends, relatives and coworkers: Teachers make a difference so try to land a good one, complain when things go wrong, don't be too understanding of the shortcomings, ask for changes.

What's new: homework assignments posted on Web sites; e-mail communications between parents and teachers.

The Limitations Of The School

The school is responsible for the education of all the students. You (the parent) are responsible for the education of your son or daughter. In many instances, sometimes all instances, the two goals are the same. What is good for your children is good for all the children. But there are clashes.

If your child is assigned a teacher of dubious skills, the school may not be able to switch the kid to a new teacher. It is highly unlikely that school will be able to fire the teacher. Or transfer the teacher to another school. This is simply the reality of civil service and the union contract.

Don't expect a call from the principal along these lines,

"Hi, Mrs. Jones. I just thought I would ring to let you know that your child has landed the worst teacher in the district. A real lulu! Nothing I can do about it, of course. I hope you have better luck next year. Bye, bye."

Just not done. Because of libel and slander laws, principals and administrators or board members can say nothing derogatory in public against school personnel.

If your school has many interim teachers or teachers with emergency credentials, it is highly unlikely it will be able to transfer a few to other schools in exchange for experienced teachers. Again the union contract, which reflects the wishes of the teachers.

Teacher Quality

What bugs many parents is not that some teachers are incompetent. California teachers number about 310,000. Of course, some are going to be failures.

Rather, parents get upset because it's very hard for a school to get rid of — never mind a mediocre teacher — sometimes even a painfully obvious incompetent.

How many teachers fall into this category? Impossible to know. We, the authors, occasionally ask our teacher friends about this. For the extremes, one said, 10 percent in her district, another said that every teacher in her district, to her knowledge, was hard working. Many people who think they would like to be teachers drop out or are weeded out before they win tenure. The profession attracts many who genuinely like kids and just about every adult will remember a beloved teacher or teachers.

Scores are misleading indicators of teacher quality. Many low-scoring schools have excellent teachers and run well-conceived, efficient programs. This is widely recognized in education. Schools have to start where the kids are and if the kids are unprepared, the scores will often be low.

But not to gloss over the problem of bad teachers; they are out there.

Also good teachers who may not be as competent as they should be. Our society is loaded with liberal arts graduates. What we're short of and what the schools have difficulty recruiting are graduates who majored in math and the sciences or who can speak Spanish fluently.

The unions insist upon uniform salary scales. Never mind demand, the science whiz gets paid as much as the English major. This may erode the quality in some classes.

What To Do

First, you should realize the principals and the staff probably will know who the incompetents are. They also know that assignments have to be made. Often, these are worked out between the principal and the teachers. Or tradition or seniority takes over. Ms. X has always taught the third grade; so she gets the third grade.

If you know who should be avoided, ask for another teacher. Don't make accusations. Just say, "I think Susie or Jose will do better with Ms. X." The principal will often go along.

If she doesn't, ask for a meeting and say something like, "I'm concerned that this will not be a good fit and want you to know that I will be watching this situation closely and I would like you to watch it." In other words, run up the warning flag.

Keep in mind that the teacher you consider incompetent may in reality just be incompatible with your child's personality or with your approach to education or your expectations.

If the school is small and has only one or two third-grade classes, the principal may not be able to oblige. You may have to make up the shortcomings at home or pay for a tutor. Or you might be able to work with the teacher to do a better job.

How do you identify the incompetent or the possibly incompetent? No method is 100 percent certain. You can chat with other parents and get their informal assessment — a good reason to get active in the school.

A fairly new Web site allows students to rate their teachers. Click on www.ratemyteachers.com.

You can check out the teacher's credential on www.teachercred.ctc.ca.gov. Or ask the school district to let you review and verify the credentials; they are public record.

The School Accountability Report Card (SARC, see Chapter 1) should tell you how many teachers at a particular school are credentialed and noncredentialed.

Look at the school or class scores. Often these are misleading but they can't be ignored.

Complain

Advice from a former teacher, now an administrator.

"Removing a teacher can be a time-consuming, expensive ordeal. The principal will often not make it a high priority unless parents complain. If enough parents complain, action might be taken."

Complaining also puts the principal and administration on notice — the parents are paying attention and are unhappy; maybe we should do a better job of hiring.

There are steps short of dismissal. The simplest: "Miss X, we are getting many complaints from parents about your teaching skills. Are you sure this is the profession for you? You might be happier doing something else."

Some teachers will agree and give it up.

Or the teacher will accept remedial training or therapy.

Or a transfer to another school in the district, if one can be found. We know of one instance where the teacher was temporarily promoted to administration. After complaining for years, the parents went public and demanded his ouster and would not back down. The district could not find a slot so into administration he went, until something could be worked out.

If a teacher is on probation, the principal can simply refuse to hire.

But if a tenured teacher digs in, the district is faced with the long and expensive fight, which it may lose. Job security is a priority with the unions and the contracts reflect this.

Sexual Misconduct, Inappropriate Actions

If you suspect that a teacher is acting inappropriately, tell the principal. If the principal's conduct is out of line, go to the superintendent.

Statewide Annual Salaries
Elementary School Districts (by size)

Statewide Average	Small	Medium	Large
Beginning Teacher	$33,848	$35,371	$37,036
Mid-range Teacher	51,197	55,531	60,113
Highest Teacher	57,748	67,900	74,006
Principal	74,087	83,242	89,875
Superintendent	94,867	115,103	138,150

High School Districts (by size)

Statewide Average	Small	Medium	Large
Beginning Teacher	$34,219	$34,902	$36,493
Mid-range Teacher	48,243	56,622	59,875
Highest Teacher	61,323	70,431	73,992
Principal	75,338	85,352	88,392
Superintendent	97,917	114,786	149,543

Unified School Districts (by size)

Statewide Average	Small	Medium	Large
Beginning Teacher	$33,290	$35,344	$35,980
Mid-range Teacher	49,210	55,581	57,139
Highest Teacher	59,743	69,990	73,953
Principal	75,264	86,279	100,810
Superintendent	94,180	131,273	171,096

Source: California Department of Education, 2001-2002.

These figures do not include benefits which vary from district to district. In 2003 and 2004, some districts, facing bankruptcy, won salary reductions from the teachers. These cutbacks are not reflected in the above numbers.

There are procedures to handle these complaints. Follow them. State law requires school districts to take these complaints seriously and investigate them.

All teachers and school employees are designated by law as "mandated reporters," meaning they must report to either the local or school district police any signs of child abuse involving a pupil. Proof of abuse is not required to make the report.

Watch what you say in public. Not every accusation has merit. The laws of libel and slander can apply, painfully, to you.

School Rhetoric

Schools and principals are not passive organizations or people. With few exceptions, they do try to solve or ameliorate personnel problems. They try to make good hires and respond to parental complaints or wishes. They have a hierarchy: Orders are handed down, from the principals, the board, the department of education. If orders are not obeyed, this could lead to dismissal.

But in many areas — and personnel is one — power is diffused throughout the system. It's not just a matter of the contract and the civil service procedures although they are very important. In elections for the school board, the union often will be the only organized group interested in the voting. Even if it puts up only a little money, this little can exert great influence.

Many parents like their teachers and listen to them. Parents dislike school fights. They like to see the school board and administrators and teachers work harmoniously — and, perhaps wisely, this takes the heat off of some passions. (But there are passions and the way schools are run draws heavy criticism. See Alan Bersin, in this chapter).

For these reasons, seldom is heard, especially in public, the discouraging word. Principals, knowing they have to live with the teachers and the janitors, cajole, praise, nudge, consult, and offer advice. When changes are to be made, often they are talked along (and talked and talked), until a consensus is reached.

Anything is possible but chances are excellent that a principal will not call in a deficient teacher and pound the desk and shout, "Miss X, you have got to shape up or you will be out on the street."

Miss X will call up the union representative, she will tell off the principal and nothing will get done.

How To Complain

So you are the parent and you've got a complaint and you're fuming because you think that the teacher is all wrong. Here's some advice from a veteran teacher:

"Don't attack the teacher.

"Don't assume that your child has told you everything.

"Don't say, something like, You should assign more homework.

"Rather try, How can I help Johnny get more homework.

"Put the focus on the child, on helping the child.

"Try to get a sense of the teacher's situation. Communicate. Perhaps the class is crowded and she doesn't have the time to assign and correct more homework.

"If the situation can be improved by working with the teacher, then work with the teacher.

"If it can't, talk to the principal."

One more bit of advice from this teacher.

"Warm and fuzzy is nice but go for the teacher who has high expectations. If you have high expectations, the kids will meet them. Do the warm and fuzzy at home."

The Teachers' Lament

If you get to know teachers, you will discover that many feel slighted and undervalued by the public. Teachers, with sound reasons, believe that for relatively small salaries, they are performing a vital task: educating the children of the country.

Not a few of them think that if kids were more respectful, if they behaved in class and simply did their homework, if parents got off their behinds and shut off the television and read to the children, a great deal more could be accomplished.

Teachers believe that too much is spent on administration and too little on facilities.

And that teachers get the blame when the school administration adopts programs that are bound to fail.

Another shortcoming: the feds and states mandate programs and refuse to pay for them.

Counselors, Psychologists, Career Technicians

Duties will vary by district.

Counselors advise the students on what classes or programs to take. If a student is unhappy with a class setting, the counselor might help her find a different program. Example: Susie is enrolled in a regular program but likes the arts. The counselor might arrange a transfer to an arts program.

Counselors try to correct behavior problems — kids cutting up in class or getting into fights or acting the bully. Sometimes the counselor will call in the parents to discuss the problem and make suggestions. If a teacher suspects a child is being abused, she might contact the counselor who might make initial inquiries and refer the matter to some specialist. The same with some learning problems — screen and refer. Advice for pregnant students, medical referrals, a shoulder to cry on, crisis to be resolved — the counselor. Some counselors join with teachers to present classes on how parents can work with the schools. (Adult schools often offer parenting classes.)

Counselors are college graduates who take a two-year program to secure a certificate in school counseling. They are generally paid the same salaries as teachers and are represented by the same unions.

School psychologists are college graduates who take a three-year program to secure a certificate in their specific field. They earn slightly more than counselors and may have their own bargaining unit.

Psychologists work with deeply emotionally disturbed children and often their families. Sometimes they intervene in family situations to protect the child. When a child or a teacher dies, the psychologist may provide grief counseling. After Sept. 11, psychologists visited campuses, listened to the students and answered questions. For severe problems, psychologists will refer the student for testing for a more precise diagnosis and try to identify an appropriate educational setting. Psychologists help evaluate children for special education.

Career Technicians. Some high schools use their counselors to advise on college entrance requirements and vocational careers. Others might use career technicians, a classified position, to dig out this material and answer questions.

Librarians, Reading Specialists, Aides

Schools may employ professional librarians who often do some teaching in the library. Reading specialists are teachers who receive extra training in reading instruction. If a child is having trouble reading, he might be pulled out of class for six or eight weeks and assigned to a reading specialist. Many parents volunteer in classes as aides. Some schools will have paid aides.

What Teacher Shortage

Not too long ago, teachers were in short supply. Between 1999 and say 2001, when the state was flush with money and schools were lowering class sizes, schools were desperate for teachers. Many people turned up their noses at teaching because the private sector was roaring along.

Now, money is tight, the private sector is crawling along and this has prompted some to reconsider teaching as a career, which alleviated the shortage.

And school enrollments in many parts of the state are falling.

Right after World War II, up to about 1958, the U.S. boomed with babies who grew up in the 1970 and 1980s and had their babies. Now the baby-boom generation, hitting 50 and 55, has said, No more!

In 1990, California recorded 611,666 births. In 2001, despite a big increase in population, births numbered 527,371, a decrease of 84,295.

Many schools districts, especially in Northern California, have stopped hiring and some are laying off. The hardest hit are located in mature towns that are built out and have priced young families out of the market. Or counties like Santa Cruz that are building few new homes.

The school districts that are hiring can be more selective.

Some districts are encouraging long-time teachers to take a buyout and replacing them with young teachers. The old are being paid at the top of the scale, the young at the bottom.

Many teachers are expected to retire in this decade and this will revive the teacher market. But for a few years, the state may be up to its hips in would-be Mr. Chips.

Teacher's Salary Schedule
Sample From Mid-sized District

Years	Bachelor's Degree Only	Bachelor's + 15 Semester Units	Bachelor's + 30 Semester Units
1	$40,222	$40,223	$40,224
2	40,223	40,224	40,225
3	40,224	40,225	40,234
4	40,225	40,234	42,293
5	40,234	42,293	44,361
6	42,293	44,361	46,428
7	44,361	46,428	48,506
8	46,428	48,506	50,573
9	48,506	50,573	52,640
10	48,506	52,640	54,727
11	48,506	52,640	56,784
12	48,506	52,640	56,784

Years	Bachelor's + 45 Semester Units	BA/S + 60 Semester Units	BA/S + 75 Semester Units
1	$40,225	$40,234	$42,293
2	40,234	42,293	44,361
3	42,293	44,361	46,428
4	44,361	46,428	48,506
5	46,428	48,506	50,573
6	48,506	50,573	52,640
7	50,573	52,640	54,727
8	52,640	54,727	56,784
9	54,727	56,784	58,850
10	56,784	58,850	60,928
11	58,850	60,928	62,999
12	60,928	62,999	65,066

Note: Teachers who are not fully credentialled earn less.

Type of Degree	Degree Stipend	Degree Total
Masters	$856	$856
Doctorate	856	1,712

*Note: Teachers also earn benefits — medical, dental, eye — in addition to salaries. Benefits vary by district.

Extracurricular Pay
Sample From Mid-sized District

Assignment	Amount	Assignment	Amount
Agriculture Judging Team	$2,323	Gymnastics, Asst.	$1,860
Aquacade Director	2,090	Gymnastics, Head	2,440
Band Director (H.S.)	2,672	Gymnastics, JV	1,976
Band/Orchestra (Mid. Sch.)	2,090	Musical (H.S. Stage/Chorus)	1,510
Baseball, Asst. Varsity	2,208	Musical (H.S. Orchestra)	1,510
Baseball, Freshman	2,265	Newspaper (H.S.)	929
Baseball, Head JV	2,382	Orchestra (H.S.)	1,510
Baseball, Head Varsity	3,077	Soccer, Head Varsity	2,496
Basketball (Mid. Sch.)	1,860	Soccer, JV	2,265
Basketball (6th grade)	1,000	Softball, Head Varsity	3,077
Basketball, Freshman	2,208	Softball, JV	2,382
Basketball, Head JV	2,382	Spirit Squad Advisor (H.S.)	2,905
Basketball, Head Varsity	3,077	Swimming, Asst.	2,033
Chorus (H.S.)	1,860	Swimming, Head	2,496
Cross Country, Head	2,033	Tennis, Asst.	1,628
Debate (H.S./Intersch.)	1,510	Tennis, Head	2,033
Drama (H.S.)	2,440	Track (Mid. Sch.)	1,628
Drama (Mid. Sch.)	1,628	Track, Asst.	2,208
Football (Mid. Sch.)	1,976	Track, Head Varsity	2,848
Football, Asst. Freshman	1,860	Volleyball (Mid. Sch.)	1,860
Football, Asst. JV	2,208	Volleyball, Head	2,208
Football, Asst. Varsity	2,496	Volleyball, Head JV	1,860
Football, Head Freshman	2,033	Water Polo	2,448
Football, Head JV	2,496	Wrestling (Mid. Sch.)	2,090
Football, Head Varsity	3,137	Wrestling, Head Varsity	2,848
Golf, Head	2,033	Wrestling, JV	2,382
Golf (Mid. Sch.)	1,000	Yearbook Advisor	1,628
Gymnastics (Mid. Sch.)	1,976		

Annual Longevity Pay For High-School Coaches

Coaching in District	Extra
3 years	$283
6 years	$566
9 years	$849
12 years	$1,132

Average Salaries by State
Public School Teachers

Rank	State	Salary	Rank	State	Salary
1	California	$54,348	27	New Hampshire	$39,915
2	Connecticut	53,551	28	Idaho	39,591
3	New Jersey	53,192	29	Florida	39,275
4	Michigan	52,676	30	Vermont	39,240
5	New York	52,000	31	Texas	39,232
6	Pennsylvania	50,599	32	Tennessee	38,515
7	Massachusetts	50,293	33	Iowa	38,230
8	Rhode Island	49,758	34	Missouri	37,996
9	Illinois	49,435	35	Kentucky	37,951
10	Alaska	49,418	36	Wyoming	37,837
11	Delaware	48,363	37	Utah	37,414
12	Maryland	48,251	38	Maine	37,300
13	Oregon	46,081	39	Alabama	37,194
14	Indiana	44,195	40	Kansas	37,093
15	Georgia	44,073	41	Arkansas	36,962
16	Ohio	44,029	42	West Virginia	36,751
17	Washington	43,464	43	New Mexico	36,440
18	North Carolina	42,680	44	Louisiana	36,328
19	Hawaii	42,615	45	Nebraska	36,236
20	Wisconsin	42,232	46	Oklahoma	34,744
21	Minnesota	42,194	47	Montana	34,379
22	Virginia	41,731	48	Mississippi	32,295
23	Nevada	40,764	49	North Dakota	32,253
24	Colorado	40,659	50	South Dakota	31,295
25	Arizona	39,973	•	Washington D.C.	47,049
26	South Carolina	39,923	•	**U.S. Average**	44,683

Source: National Education Assn. Research, 2001-2002. Some entries are estimates.
Does not include benefits, which vary widely.

Cost of Living

Trying to factor in the cost of living, one union concluded that a California teacher earning $47,680 a year had, compared to other teachers in the nation, the "buying power" of $38,845. According to this study, a teacher earning $45,103 in Oregon, where living is cheaper, enjoyed a buying power of $47,652. Within California, salaries and benefits vary widely by district.

Battling Bersin of San Diego

Alan Bersin, by the battles he has waged, has brought to the surface many of the arguments that rage in educational circles but rarely come to the attention of the public.

Bersin is the superintendent of the San Diego district, 142,000 students. In 1998, the San Diego business community, local Republicans and civic leaders, disappointed by the quality of graduates, lobbied the school board to hire someone to shake up the district. In came Bersin, corporate lawyer and former U.S. Attorney with no experience in education.

About two years before he arrived, the teachers' union, after a strike, convinced the district to push decision making down to the schools and into the hands of teachers, parents and community representatives. Many people in education would consider this the ideal arrangement — power to those closest to the students, decisions by consensus of those most involved, teachers at the head of the table.

But under this model, accountability was difficult. If a bad decision was made, it was hard to discipline those in charge. If a program was not working (but supplied jobs and had supporters), it might be left unchanged to keep the peace. And, in fact, this seemed be happening. Although the district had about 200 reading programs, many students were graduating barely able to read or write.

Bersin approached the district as if it were a business. He demoted 15 principals, slimmed the central bureaucracy and dissolved the 200 programs and replaced them with a comprehensive program. He hired an expert from New York City to install a system to train and evaluate teachers and paid him an annual salary of about $900,000 — something common in business but almost unheard of in K-12 education.

The union rebelled. It argued that teachers should evaluate and train teachers, that one training system did not fit all, that independent-minded teachers might be punished. Bersin's methods, others contended, implied that teachers were at least part of the problem — which the teachers resented.

There ensued a long battle with the teachers union, in one election, spending $500,000 to win control of the school board. Bersin survived but the arguments continued.

Who's right? Hard to know. Common to many arguments over education, both sides made points that sound logical. On some key issues they agreed: more training for teachers. Even if the union defeated Bersin and his program, the school district would still have had to come up an accountability program to meet state and federal requirements.

Bersin became a hero to many who think the schools should set and enforce clearly defined standards and that managers should have the power at least to eliminate programs that are not working.

This fight ties into other questions being debated around the U.S. They include:

• The power of the unions. To many conservatives, the unions, with their rules and job guarantees, are the bane of public education. This belief fuels many of the arguments in education and many of the controversial changes, notably vouchers and charter schools. The conservatives argue that the unions see money as the salvation of the schools but refuse to make structural changes that might help the students.

The unions counter that they and their members are being blamed unfairly, that teachers deserve adequate salaries, and that many of the problems are due to lack of funds and the presence of so many children poorly prepared for school.

• Better training. Business people, politicians, educators — almost everyone agrees that trained teachers are more effective than untrained. The feds, under No Child Left Behind, are saying that by 2006 all classrooms should be led by "highly qualified" teachers. In California, this means certificated teachers.

Many consider this an impossible deadline but California districts are becoming more insistent about the credential.

Some people applaud the idea of better training but past a certain point prefer accountability and incentives. They would judge and reward teachers not by the courses they took but by their performance in the classroom and by test scores.

• *Accountability and Job Security.* *The new testing methods are inching toward a system that may allow schools to do a better job of assessing teacher performance. The No-Child laws appear to be pushing failing schools toward the private sector or to charters. The unions oppose funding for private schools and are wary of charters, suspecting they might be weakening the union contract.*

• *The role of the unions.* *In California and elsewhere, the unions clearly are big-time players. They contribute heavily to the Democratic party and work with state officials on budget matters. In 2004, they sat down with Governor Arnold Schwarzenegger and hammered out a compromise on funding for the K-12 system. Behind the scenes, unions advance not only the financial interests of the teachers but, through legislation introduced by usually Democratic legislators, the academic changes the teachers would like to see in the system.*

Yet the unions rarely step into the spotlight and the public, while professing to love teachers individually, seem to distrust the unions. In 2003, public opposition shot down a proposal to give California teachers, through their unions, more power to choose textbooks and determine curriculum.

•*Possible Changes* *If you're interested in what changes might be made in California schools, take a look at The California Master Plan for Education. It can be downloaded by searching on the title. The plan, which is being put together by a state legislative committee, gives a good review of California education and presents dozens of recommendations.*

Looping

Your kid just started second grade. So guess who's there to greet her? Her second-grade teacher, the same teacher she had in first grade and likely will have in third grade

Looping keeps the same pupils with the same teacher over several years instead of moving to new teachers and classrooms every year. The intent, educators say, is to boost achievement and give the kids, especially at large schools, a sounder footing in a familiar setting. Teachers already know their pupils and don't have to spend time learning their abilities. If you don't like the teacher, ask for a new one.

4

Curriculum and Standards
College Prep,
Grad Requirements

Over the last 10-15 years and especially in the last few years, California has overhauled its basic curriculum and made it much easier to understand. More changes are coming, along with, naturally, arguments.

When you visit your child's school on Back-to-School-Night and Open House, you will get a good dose of Accountability, the collective name for the overhaul. It is also called Direct Instruction or the Academic Performance Index (API) or No-Child Left Behind or Standards and Assessments. There are differences between the variations, which we will sort out later in this chapter.

You will also encounter accountability in report cards and in test results and in many media stories. It's a big deal.

One point to keep in mind — the basic curriculum is not the college-prep curriculum. They mesh. A good grounding in the basics will always prove helpful in the college prep. But in several key ways the college prep differs from the basic.

How We Got To Basic

In the 1960s, our universities, schools and other institutions took up in earnest a question that has always fascinated Americans — what's the best way to teach the children, or What Works.

The context was the civil rights revolution and the harm done by centuries of prejudice and oppression. Many people embraced the idea that the schools, with new programs and more money, would quickly raise the scores of disadvantaged children and allow them to graduate into better jobs and a better life.

One of the first big programs, Head Start, took the children at a young age and prepared them for kindergarten and the first grade — preschool.

Very soon researchers concluded that Head Start was not a breakthrough. The program still has many supporters but its critics call it a failure.

Other programs or approaches were introduced — new math, whole language, open classrooms, self esteem, decentralized schools, magnet schools, alternative schools, and so on. And a discouraging truth emerged:

Just because a program was logical and clever and taught by experienced and enthusiastic teachers did not mean that it would succeed.

Some solutions advanced the students in one year only to see them surrender their gains a few years later.

Some helped a few students but not large groups.

Some programs tested well in one state but not in others. California recently had a example of this. It embraced low enrollments in grades kindergarten through three because this practice in other states had raised scores. But in California, the practice has brought mixed results; some schools up, some down.

Some argued, well, California hired too many teachers, too fast, and that's why results were not forthcoming. And they may be right; the jury is still out on this one. But, here again is another illustration of the difficulty of figuring out what works.

Fights Break Out

Billions were invested in the new ideas and programs. Many of them found their way into the regular classrooms. And once in, became hard to dislodge. Teachers were trained in the new methods. Funding got caught up in political battles. Jobs came with the funding — an important consideration. In many towns and counties, school districts are the number one employer.

In the 1970s and 1980s, as the disappointments became common, battles broke out over what works and who was to blame.

Conservatives took after liberals and the unions and argued that reform was impossible until parents had choice of schools and the power of the unions was broken. The teachers' unions countered that the real problems were miserly funding and the failure of parents to prepare their children for school.

A few cities and states turned to vouchers, which allow parents restricted choice of private schools; religious schools are not acceptable for vouchers.

California, in the ballot box, said no to vouchers but embraced the charter method, which allows parents and local groups to open their own public schools free of many regulations that apply to public schools. See Chapter 7.

Many of these fights were probably inevitable. The country had great expectations for the new programs and had we not tried them, we would have been kicking ourselves for ignoring what seemed to be very workable. The fights still rage. There is something about education that seems to rile people. But about 1990, exhausted after the failures, many educators, parents, business leaders and others became more "prove it" about new programs.

A Key Study

In the late 1960s, the federal government commissioned a study on what worked in the early grades. Researchers studied nine ways of teaching the children and in 1977 released their findings. The most effective — and its champions argue, the only effective model — was one called Direct Instruction.

Direct Instruction and its close variations are structured and employ many techniques that can accurately be described as old fashioned. Direct Instruction divides skills and material into small units and drills the children on these units. It uses a lot of repetition, repetition, repetition. It uses tests. One signature technique: phonics: breaking words into letters and sounds as opposed to immersion or whole language where the pupil learns by reading a passage and trying to understand the words by their context.

Other studies followed and they also gave good marks to Direct Instruction but many educators resisted the program.

Some arguments: Direct Instruction was simple minded and did not equip students with the complex skills they need in modern society. These skills could not be measured by standardized tests. Direct Instruction diminished the role of the teacher and brought back "drill and kill" techniques that supposedly had been discredited. The fight continues.

The Rise of Direct Instruction

In the 1990s, Direct Instruction or its variations won out, not only in California but in many other states. Because Direct Instruction had done well in the studies, it could boast academic credibility. It was grounded in tradition and in old and respected practices within American business. Anyone familiar with Total Quality Management will have no trouble recognizing Direct Instruction. It became one of the favorites of the Republican Party in an era when the Republicans controlled Congress and the White House. President George W. Bush is one of its biggest fans.

Many Democrats also went for the approach. One of its strongest supporters was Delaine Eastin, California superintendent of schools for most of the 1990s and a Democrat. The new superintendent, Jack O'Connell, supports accountability.

In 1999, the California Legislature, dominated by Democrats, passed legislation that installed many of the accountability tools recently — or soon to be — put into practice. In California, the bureaucracy prefers the term, accountability or standards and assessments or Academic Performance Index (API), instead of Direct Instruction.

How Accountability Works

It's a system. It's not confined to one school or several districts. It is applied to almost every school in the state but many schools, as we will explain, can ignore its penalties and its stricter methods. Here are the main characteristics:

- **Clear definitions.** The California Department of Education has defined what students should be learning in school — the basic curriculum, grade by grade, in detail. You can view the curriculum on the department of education Web site, www.cde.gov, or obtain it from your local school. To get some idea of what the curriculum looks like, see the back of this chapter.

  When parents go to back-to-school night or parent conferences, teachers will present the state standards-curriculum and tell you how well your child is doing in mastering this material.

- **Textbooks and Teaching Materials.** Many have been rewritten to bring them in line with the standards and curriculum. This doesn't mean that they have invented facts or made two plus two equal five. It means, for example, that textbooks cover the topics presented in the class.

- **Teacher training and techniques.** Teachers are expected to tie their lesson plans and goals to the state standards and curriculum. At some schools, the lessons may be scripted; that is, the teachers may read directly from a manual and follow the state schedule (which is why some teachers despise Direct Instruction; it curtails their flexibility to work with students as they see fit.) But many other schools retain their flexibility to meet the standards.
- **Test alignment.** Here are two old complaints: The off-the-shelf tests used by the state quizzed the kids on material that was not covered in class. And, students studied for the test at the expense of material that should have been covered in class.

  With accountability, the tests are aligned — or are being aligned — to the curriculum and material used in the classroom.

  Test results are broken out for individual students and for schools. See Chapter 5, Tests.
- **More tests.** Testing is a key part of accountability. The tests are used to identify student and program weaknesses, so they can be corrected, and to penalize failure and reward achievement, or put some incentives into the system. As of 2004, high-school students will be required to pass an algebra test. In 2006, they will be required to pass an exit exam.

  Many of the tests are done informally. One example from a Southern California district: Students at their own speed read books or chapters, then take a short test that is immediately scored by computer. Result: quick feed back on what they know.
- **Some muscling up of the basic curriculum.** For example, the addition of algebra as a graduation requirement.
- **Goals.** School scores are presented in a range from 200 to 1,000 (Academic Performance Index — API.) The goal is to get all the California schools and their subgroups scoring at 800 (by year 2014).
- **Targets or Benchmarks.** It is unlikely that a school scoring 500 will jump to 800 within a year. For this reason, schools every year are assigned a benchmark or interim target and asked to hit the target.
- **Reward and penalties.** If a school does not hit its targets for two years in a row, it can be penalized. The state is approaching

penalties in one way, the feds in another way — major arguments. See following:

Until California ran out of money, it was rewarding teachers and schools with cash bonuses for big leaps in the scores. Now, it's a pat on the back, public recognition, and some incentives that help schools win achievement awards.

- **Public and Parental Awareness.** In the not-so-old days, reports on student and school progress were often vague. Now they are fairly precise and focused on achievement. See Chapter 5, Tests.

NO EXCUSES SPELLING LIST

Schools can set informal requirements. Here's one from a Southern California district. "The following list of words must be spelled and used correctly by all students. Students will be held accountable for the correct spelling of the following words in EVERY class on our campus."

1. accept
2. except
3. affect
4. effect
5. all right
6. a lot
7. approval
8. boycott
9. can't
10. Capistrano
11. conscious
12. conscience
13. could have
14. definite
15. develop
16. development
17. exhilaration
18. grammar
19. guidance
20. illegible
21. incoherent
22. indefinite
23. its
24. it's
25. literature
26. peace
27. piece
28. playwright
29. principal
30. principle
31. recommendation
32. receive
33. sentence
34. separate
35. should have
36. sincerely
37. sophomore
38. than
39. then
40. their
41. there
42. they're
43. to
44. too
45. tragedy
46. transcript
47. truly
48. two
49. through
50. vertical
51. weird
52. we're
53. where
54. won't
55. would have
56. your
57. you're

No Child Left Behind

In 2002, the federal government passed sweeping legislation called No Child Left Behind or NCLB (another bit of jargon becoming popular in education).

In many ways, the No-Child law is one and the same with the California accountability legislation passed in 1999.

No Child left it to the individual states to define their own standards and assessments and benchmarks and then incorporated them into the No-Child law.

In other words, California's standards are also the federal standards.

Where the California accountability law and the federal No-Child law differ is mainly in penalties and in the failings that trigger the penalties.

Broadly speaking, the California law nudges, cajoles, embarrasses and pressures the local school districts into making improvements.

When a school fails for several years running, the state may assign an intervention team or force the transfer of the principal and its staff.

If the school continues to fail, the California law requires the department of education to do one — only one — of the following:

• Allow transfers to schools with space but parents pay cost of transportation.

• Allow parents to change the failing school into a charter institution.

• Assign management of the school to a college or university or county office of education.

• Close or reorganize the school.

• Reassign other certificated personnel (teachers) but in accordance with union contracts.

• Negotiate a new contract with the teachers' union but only after the existing contract expired.

There are other actions that can be taken after holding meetings and making "findings" and taking steps that could drag on for years.

The state plan set targets for schools and for categories — ethnic groups, disadvantaged, learning disabled, limited English, etc.

The feds, through No Child, took the same targets but defined progress to a higher standard. With the state approach, failings would be few; with the federal many.

The No-Child Penalties

- **Failing two years in a row.** Parents are allowed to transfer children to other schools within the same district. School must pay for transportation (but this might amount to no more than a ticket on a public bus).
- **Failing three years in a row.** School must fund tutoring. Transfers allowed.
- **Four years failing.** School staff can be dismissed. Outside expert can be named to advise school. Longer school day or year. Transfers.
- **Five years failing.** School staff to be "reorganized." Or school turned over to charter group or private management firm.

In 2003, the state and federal penalties kicked in and people saw that the feds were serious. Failing schools receiving certain federal funds (Title 1) were told, "OK, you had your chance, now under the No-Child law you have to allow your students to transfer to other schools and you pay the transit bill."

The "other" schools were schools in the same district and they had to have space for additional students.

Many parents at the failing schools said no to the transfers or were turned down for lack of space. But a sizeable number went for the transfers and moved their kids to higher-scoring schools.

What's Next?

Keep in mind that neither the State of California nor the feds are arguing over standards and assessments or the instructional program for basics. They agree on almost everything but the penalties for failure. The overall program appears here to stay.

Short term, because all this is wrapped up in politics and ideology, you can expect a fair amount of posturing, name calling and behind-the-scenes maneuvering.

Not only California but many states are butting heads with the feds over No Child Left Behind and its penalties.

Many parts of No-Child and the state accountability program were drafted in times of budget surpluses. Now, no surpluses; instead, deep deficits. The school districts are saying, you promised us money to implement these changes and now, "You're shorting us and still insisting on penalties. No fair!"

The state will continue to enforce its accountability penalties. No one seems upset about them.

At least for the short term, the federal transfer policy will probably stay in effect. If your child attends a "failing" school and you want out, here's your chance. Talk to your school officials and see what schools in your district (or even other districts) are accepting transfers.

The Exit Exam — Penalty Pressure

Other provisions include increasing graduation rates and putting more credentialed teachers in the schools.

Then there is the exit exam, delayed several times, and scheduled to be put into play in 2006.

Here's a way to look at penalties. All the stuff that we have laid out in the preceding paragraphs puts pressure on the schools and administrators and, indirectly, the teachers.

The exit exam puts pressure on the students. If they don't pass the exam, they don't get the "real" high-school diploma and this might hurt their chances to land a job.

How Accountability Plays Out In Schools

If the program succeeds as hoped, California students, scores low to high, will get a stronger grounding in the basics. Those who don't need it might find it a waste of time and the system sort of acknowledges this and makes some allowances. Those who do — and this includes many students who are college bound — probably will find this beneficial.

If your school is scoring above the 800 mark or close to it, the state has all but said it will not bother these schools. Almost all the attention is going to low- and middle-scoring schools.

High-scoring schools, however, do not escape academic pressure. Their discipline comes from the college-prep curriculum and college-entrance exams. See College Prep in this chapter.

If your school is scoring above the 800 mark but failing in one of its categories, the state may review the academic program for this category and make some recommendations. The feds may allow transfers but it is unlikely that many parents will go this route. The choice is ... what? Transfer to a lower-scoring school. The parents will probably stay put and work with the high-scoring school.

As for schools scoring low to middle, theoretically, they can meet the standards any way they want and in fact schools are meeting them in a variety ways — Montessori, long-day, charter flexibility, regular instruction and so on.

But especially where scores are low, some, possibly many, schools are favoring very structured methods to help their kids. This is where the so-called scripting may be entering. The school district is saying to the teachers: this way works, we want you to use it.

At least a few districts, notably San Diego Unified and Los Angeles, have worked out detailed programs to meet the standards.

In schools, where scores are middling to high, teachers may be given more flexibility to meet the standards. One scenario described by a teacher: she and her colleagues get together to discuss the standards and how to coordinate lesson plans. The teacher executes the lesson plan but finds extra or different material for children who are doing well with the basics.

Incidentally, several of the elementary teachers whom we talked to said they mixed phonics with whole language because some kids respond to one and some to the other. There still is an active tradition of using what the teacher thinks will work (and some research favors this mix.)

Low- and middle-scoring schools may sacrifice other parts of the regular curriculum to raise reading and math scores. See following on science.

For parents who want to keep on top of their kids' education, the new system may prove very helpful. It really does spell out what the kids should know at each grade level. Some of the material slogs into jargon (see end of this chapter) but book publishers are coming to the rescue with easily understood books on the new standards. Visit your local bookstore.

Science Classes And What's Enforced

State law requires schools to teach science in the elementary grades but many don't or teach very little or make science an elective.

This shortcoming illustrates one of the quirks of California education. Even though a certain subject is required, if the state does not enforce its order, the subject may not be offered.

For the present, the state is enforcing reading, writing and math. Many schools, especially the low-scoring, are concentrating on these subjects. If they fail in these subjects, the schools will be punished or embarrassed or inconvenienced.

If they fail to offer science, there is no punishment. So many of these schools are not offering science.

This is where pacing (see scores chapter) and overall scores enter. If a school has mastered the basics, it can carve out time for other subjects, including science.

The state has drawn up a science curriculum. If you want to see what you're child should be learning, ask the school for this curriculum or download it from the California Dept. of Education Web site: www.cde.gov.

Science courses have to be offered at the high school because they are part of the college-prep curriculum. (See graduation and college-prep requirements in this chapter.)

Many people are pushing the state to make science a true part of the curriculum. Or they are nudging their local districts to take action. Many times it's easier to win the local battle as opposed to the state fight.

The San Diego district, the second largest in the state, recently made physics a graduation requirement for its high-school students. San Diego came up with two physics classes, one (without a lot of math and without trigonometry) for slow and average students, the other for the top students — a compromise that nonetheless had opponents. The district had to hire 23 teachers good in science and start the program with many teachers unskilled in the subject (but some were taking science classes at the local university.)

Art, Music And Performing Arts

In the elementary grades, if the school has the time and the money, it will usually offer art and music. If these subjects are not offered, however, the school is not punished.

With the new accountability standards, which elevate reading, writing and math, more schools may find it difficult to field art and music or may have to reduce their efforts.

Parents interested in these pursuits may have to raise funds to get them offered or lobby the school board. Or pay for private lessons.

Many parents, and indeed probably most Californians, want the schools to offer music and art and acting to the young kids. But money and time are problems.

Almost all high schools field a band and offer art. In recent years, many large school districts have turned one or several high schools into performing arts institutions. These schools offer the core curriculum and load up on theater and arts pursuits.

For those who think this sounds like fluff, keep in mind that entertainment is a big industry in California and the West (Hollywood, Reno and Las Vegas).

Foreign Languages

All high schools with a college-prep program will offer classes in a foreign language. Students are required to take these classes to gain admission to a university (or take them in community college).

Language programs almost invariably will include Spanish. It's the second language of California. Other popular offerings include French and Chinese. And to a lesser extent, Latin, Korean and

German. If many students attending a certain high school come from a particular ethnic group, the school might offer their language, especially if parents request it. Or the school might help form a club that cultivates that language.

To find out what language classes are offered, ask for the school catalog.

Language Classes In Elementary Grades

In the elementary grades (and to a lesser extent, the high schools), language instruction has been dragged into the fight over what's the best way to teach immigrant students or students who speak a foreign language at home and need to improve their English.

For well over a decade, California used a method followed by many other urban states: Start the kids in their native language, then introduce them to English and by the fourth or fifth grade move them into English fluency.

Sounds logical and makes sense but for reasons that are still being argued vehemently, the bilingual approach didn't work as well as expected. At the end of the fifth grade, not only in California but elsewhere, many students were speaking little English.

The revolt in California took the form of a 1998 initiative that severely curtailed bilingual classes and boosted English only. There followed court cases and appeals to the state Board of Education and reworkings of the language classes. The arguments continue and more changes probably will be made but they may not be big.

Parents have choices. In most instances, the school will present the choices and ask your permission to place the child in a language class.

Policies will vary by district. In districts with few non-English speaking students, there may be only classes in English. Or the help for limited-English students may be confined to lower grades.

Instruction techniques will also vary. Over the years, there has been a lot of trial and error in bilingual ed. Textbooks have been revised and new ways of teaching introduced.

Here are some terms that, we hope, will clarify matters:

• **English Language Learners.** This is an umbrella term that covers any child who needs to learn or improve his English and is enrolled in some kind of program. The old term, which is still is wide use, is English as a Second Language or ESL.

• **Alternative Bilingual.** Under the old method, the children were educated in their native language and as they grew older were introduced to English. With alternative bilingual, students may be required to spend the first six weeks of school year in English-only classes and then allowed to transfer into a bilingual class. Within the classroom, English is introduced earlier. A first grade may spend 90 percent in the native language and 10 percent in English, and in the second year move to an 80-20 ratio and so on.

• **Structured English immersion.** Students are taught in English for one year but receive help in native language.

• **Dual Immersion.** Students are taught half in native language and half in English or close variation. These classes, to avoid running afoul of the law, have to enroll roughly one English-speaking student for every limited-English student. Dual immersion is used by some English-speaking parents as a way to get their children to learn a second language.

• **Mainstream.** Regular instruction; no formal help for limited-English students. Informally, the teacher, who may speak or understand a foreign language, might offer some help. "Mainstream" is often used to describe the goal, as in, "We intend to mainstream all our limited-English students within x years."

Language Test

Every year the state administers the California English Language Development Test to students identified as English Language Learners. If the student scores at what is considered fluent, she may opt out of language instruction classes. Schools use this test to advise students what language classes to take and to enroll them in certain classes. Complaints have surfaced that even when students test "fluent" some schools continue to place them in language classes. One school replied that it thought that some of its "fluent" students needed more language help to succeed in mainstream classes. In these situation, parents should talk to school officials.

What Can Schools Teach About AIDS?

AIDS or acquired immune deficiency syndrome must, by state law, be taught to every student in grades seven through 12. Unless a parent objects to the class, the student will take the class once in middle or junior high and once again in high school.

Instruction includes:

• The nature of AIDS and its effects on the human body.

• How AIDS is transmitted.

• Methods of reducing the risk of infection including abstinence and condoms.

• Public health issues associated with AIDS.

• Local resources for HIV (human immunodeficiency virus, the virus that causes AIDS) testing and treatment.

• How to avoid high-risk activities.

• Discussions of community views about AIDS and HIV-positive people.

Sex Education Classes?

Again, as with AIDS, parents can request not to have their child participate.

What Is Taught In Sex Education Or "Family Life"

The law:

"No governing board of a public elementary or secondary school may require pupils to attend any class in which human reproductive organs and their functions and processes are described, illustrated or discussed, whether such class be part of a course designated 'sex education' or 'family life education' or by some similar term, or part of any other course which pupils are required to attend.

"If [such] classes are offered ... the parent or guardian of each pupil enrolled in such class shall first be notified in writing of the class," it continues.

Abstinence must be emphasized as the only method that is 100 percent effective in preventing pregnancy, AIDS and other sexually transmitted diseases.

Sexual intercourse discussions must be "factually" accurate. Information about condoms must include the latest medical data citing their success and failure rates.

Emotional and psychological consequences of being sexually active also must be discussed along with the financial impact of teen pregnancy.

Instruction and course material must stress that students should avoid sex until they are ready for marriage. Respect for heterosexual, monogamous marriages also shall be taught.

Many schools start sex ed between the fourth and seventh grade. The school will send home a permission slip. If you want to pull your child out of the session, sign and send it back. If you want the classes, do nothing.

Parents May Review Curriculum

Parents may ask the school to be allowed to review the curriculum and also, upon a written request, to observe a particular class.

If You Don't Want To Carve The Frog

Students with moral objections to dissection may request an exemption and be given an alternate assignment without any retaliation.

Religion And Race

A student may not be forced to embrace or disavow any world view, political or religious doctrine. Schools texts can talk about religions but not endorse any creed.

Schools work at teaching the kids to get along and never mind differences in race, culture or religion. Where they can, schools celebrate this or that culture — Martin Luther King's Birthday, Cinco de Mayo — but in the spirit of respecting all cultures.

Early in 2004, France's proposal to ban certain religious headwear or symbols in its public schools made international headlines. California officials, however, say there have been no discussions of such a ban here. Any attempt likely would be challenged as an infringement of religious expression.

Community Service

Although not part of the regular curriculum, many schools, as a condition of graduation, require their students to help those in need. The students, it is hoped, will continue to do good works and take an interest in the community. Here are the requirements for one high school in Northern California.

• At least 20 hours of work, preferably 10 hours one year, 10 in another.

• Students can help children, the elderly, the disabled, the ill or injured (hospital volunteering). They can also work in shelters, soup kitchens and emergency-assistance programs. They can clean up parks, tutor, and help groom the dogs and cats at the local animal shelter. Many schools will give their students a list of organizations looking for volunteers.

Vocational Education.
See Chapter 8

Pledge Of Allegiance
Until the U.S. Supreme Court clarifies a lower court's ruling, the pledge is being recited in some schools and not in others. Check your local officials. The lower court held that the phrase "under God" violated constitutional provisions mandating church-state separation. However, reciting the pledge is voluntary. The legal dispute focuses on whether hearing "under God" violates the Constitution.

Required Subjects For Graduation
Currently a student must successfully complete all the following to earn a high-school diploma:
• Three years of English.
• Two years of math (including Algebra I).
• Three years of social science. This area requires U.S. history and geography, one semester of American government, one semester of economics, world history, culture and geography.
• Two years of science (including biology and physical science).
• Two years of physical education.
• One year of foreign language or visual and performing arts.

These are minimum standards and many districts exceed these requirements. Some districts have their pet requirements, such as a spelling list.

One San Diego County district requires all students to make a speech either during their junior or senior year. The students are graded on such things as quality of their research, effectiveness of any props or visual aids as well as on their speaking style and persuasiveness.

The K-12 Curriculum Also Includes Or Requires:
• Driver's education. Whether it is required for graduation is the district's choice.
• Parenting skills during grades seven or eight or both.
• Applied arts including consumer education and home economics, industrial arts, general business or general agriculture.

Drug And Alcohol Abuse Classes
All districts must provide such classes. What grade levels should receive them is the discretion of the local district.

Many districts offer a DARE (Drug Abuse and Resistance Education) classes, often taught by local police officers. These courses focus not only on illegal drugs and alcohol but steroids.

Driver's Education
Traffic collisions are the leading cause of teen deaths in California.

Thus the requirement that schools offer Driver's Education. Many districts offer it during the sophomore year in the health classes when students are studying such issues as drugs, alcohol and driver fatigue.

The schools provide the classroom instruction. Behind-the-wheel training is usually left to private firms. Cost about $100.

A student may secure a provisional permit at age 15.5 after passing a written test and may obtain a license at 16 after passing a behind-the-wheel test. During the first six months a teen is licensed, she must be accompanied by a licensed driver 25 years or older when carrying passengers under the age of 20. During the first year, she must be accompanied by a licensed driver 25 or older when driving between midnight and 5 a.m.

The College-Prep Curriculum

Although the high schools and the California Department of Education draw up the prep curriculum, the real power is the University of California and, indirectly, the top universities of the nation.

The University of California (UC) is the collective name of the University of California system, which governs the top universities in the state. See Chapter 2.

The UC system says to students, "If you want to attend a UC, you must take these courses, commonly known as the A-G requirements." These requirements also apply to the California State University system.

Most of the college-bound students in the state attend a UC or a California State University (Chapter 2). The high schools, public and private, would be terribly stupid to ignore the UC requirements and none do.

The UC requirements pretty much reflect what universities require around the nation.

The UC Minimum Requirements

• Four years of college preparatory English.
• Three years of math (including algebra, geometry and intermediate algebra).
• Two years of history or social science.
• Two years of laboratory science (biological and physical).
• Two years of the same foreign language.
• One year of visual or performing arts.
• One year of academic electives.

And More

The UCs take the top 12.5 percent of applicants, the Cal States the top third. If a student wants to get into a UC, he or she must take more and tougher classes.

This rule, with much argument, applies to universities nationwide: the more prestigious the university, the tougher the requirements. The UC, for example, recommends applicants take advanced courses in math, science and a foreign language.

Advanced Placement

Advanced Placement or AP classes as they're known among students and teachers are college-level courses in 21 subject areas that high school students may substitute for the regular curriculum.

Students who take AP classes often have a better chance of getting into a prestigious university.

For College Prep Information

Your local high school counseling office should be able to provide you with information about applying to universities.

For some parents, however, the local high school and its counselors are not enough. In California, there is small but flourishing bevy of college-admission gurus who specialize, for a fee, in getting your child into a good college. So complex has this business become that the UC Extension offers classes on the college-admission process. To find a college advisor, look in the phone book under Educational Consulting or ask a high school counselor.

The UC Web site www.ucop.edu/doorways/list lists the high schools and for each school details the courses certified as meeting admission standards. Admission requirements for both the UC and California State University systems are available at http://www.californiacolleges.edu.

The Basics And The College Prep

If your high-schooler is smart enough to pass the college prep classes, does she have to worry about the basics and accountability?

In many cases, no, which is one criticism of the accountability approach. It requires advanced students to take tests — the annual STAR test and the upcoming exit exam — which offer little challenge.

The challenge for these students comes with the SAT and the college admission tests.

Nonetheless, it's prudent to take a close look at the basics approach.

Research over a decade shows that about half the students admitted to California State Universities need remedial instruction in English and math. For students admitted to a University of California, about one third require remedial work in English. A student who masters the basics will have good foundation to proceed to the advanced.

Further, these tests are being revised and expanded to include such subjects as chemistry and algebra.

UC is changing its admission procedures and informally UC officials have said they would like to see the SAT, which is being revised, to do a better job of asking questions about material taught in California schools.

The new SAT, scheduled to go into service in 2006, is to give more weight to writing skills and less to analogies. The test is coming with a good deal of argument because the university and California and its residents disagree about how much flexibility the UC system should have in deciding who gets in.

California Curriculum Standards

Starting in the late 1990s, California spelled out a basic program of what the children should be learning grade by grade — the curriculum standards.

The state then ordered new textbooks and tests that were aligned to the new curriculum.

The following will give you the flavor of the curriculum and the standards. The state has posted these standards in detail on its Web site, www.cde.edu. All schools will have these standards and many schools are making extra efforts to ensure that parents understand them.

English Language

Second-grade English.

- Know common abbreviations such as Jan., Mon., Mr., Ave.
- Explain what is a complete sentence and what is an incomplete sentence.

Fourth-grade English

- Read stories and instructions aloud with grade-appropriate fluency and accuracy. Use appropriate pacing, intonations and expression.

Seventh-grade English

- Identify idioms, analogies, metaphors and similes in prose and poetry.
- Write a fictitious or autobiographical narrative that has a beginning, middle and end and has a consistent point of view.

Mathematics

Kindergarten Math

- Name and count in order a number of objects up to 30.
- Be able to use objects to demonstrate adding and subtracting numbers less than 10.

First-grade Math

- Know the value of coins and show how combinations of different coins can have the same value.

Algebra I

- Use properties of numbers to demonstrate the validity of a claim.
- Understand what parallel lines are as well as perpendicular lines and how they are related.

Algebra II

- Prove simple laws of logarithms.
- Be adept at operations on polynomials, including long division.

Geometry

- Write geometric proofs including proofs by contradiction.

Trigonometry

- Understand the notion of angle and how to measure angles in degrees and radians.
- Solve problems by applying the knowledge of sines and cosines.

Calculus

- Know Newton's method for approximating the zeros of a function.

History-Social Science Standards

First-grade History

- Use maps and globes to find hometowns, California, the United States, the seven continents and the four oceans.

Second-grade History

- Tell how our laws are made and enforced along with those of other countries.

Third-grade History

- Explain the role of geography and climate in how local Indians adapted to their surroundings.

Seventh-grade History

- Describe the effects of reopening the ancient "Silk Road," or connection between Europe and China.

Eighth-grade History

- List the government's powers contained in the Constitution and the liberties guaranteed by the Bill of Rights.

Science Standards

Second-grade Science

- Know an object's motion can be described by noting its change in position over time.

Third-grade Science

- Know that energy can be stored in batteries, food or fuel.
- Know that various animals can live in different places such as deserts, forests, wetlands and grasslands.

Fourth-grade Science

- Design and build simple series and parallel circuits from batteries, wires and bulbs.

Physics

- Know relationship between the universal law of gravitation and the effect of gravity on an object at the surface of Earth.

Chemistry

- Locate elements on the periodic table by atomic number and mass.

Biology/Life Sciences

- Know how antibodies respond to the body's infection.

Earth Sciences

- Cite evidence that planets are nearer the Earth than stars.
- Know that the age of the solar system and how it formed can be determined by analyzing moon rocks and those on earth.

Investigation and Experimentation

- Recognize the cumulative nature of scientific evidence.

Visual and Performing Arts Standards: Dance

Sixth-grade Dance

- Devise ways to overcome a specific movement problem and then apply them to a dance study.

Seventh-grade Dance

- Show the willingness and ability to assume greater risks through using more space to perform movements.

Ninth- through Twelfth-grade Dance

Proficient

- Perform a number of different types of dance from ballet, modern, jazz or recreational.
- Devise and execute a body of work emphasizing originality, intent and expression.

Advanced:

- Perform from memory dances that show a high degree of complexity and professionalism.
- Instruct fellow students in performing various complex movements.

Pomp & Circumstance

This is the moment you've been working toward since you enrolled your child in preschool— high school graduation. The traditional strains of the "Pomp and Circumstance" march are playing and your child's name is being called off to accept his diploma. Next is college, the military or work. But there's some unfinished business regarding high school. For instance, are you sure your child will graduate?

Unpaid library fines, lost books or other money matters.
Before graduation rolls around and your child isn't allowed to march in, make sure that you have checked that all the fines are paid and books are returned. Some schools will withhold the diploma but allow your child to participate in the ceremonies, others will say no greenbacks, no sheepskin and no ceremony.

Does the school have all your child's credits from other schools?
Check with your school officials, make sure all his transcripts and other necessary papers have been received. Sometimes, not often, things get lost or never are received.

Your child is graduating, then what?
If she plans to attend college, she should have applied much earlier. Many students start their college search early, even in their junior year. While they are busy taking honors or advanced placement courses and doing community service work to influence college admissions officials, the kids are pumping out application letters to more than one college.

Check with your child's counselors about colleges that might be appropriate. Go on the Internet to search the colleges' websites; many post their admissions applications and course catalogs online.

If it's work, not college, she should check with the school's placement counselors about what jobs are available and appropriate. The vocational education staff is a good starting point. It might not hurt to look into adult school or the local community college for classes that might better prepare her for a job.

Salutatorian, valedictorian. What's the difference?

In most schools, the graduating student with the highest grade-point average is selected as valedictorian, The valedictorian gives the farewell address at graduation on behalf of the graduating class. The next highest student is selected salutatorian, the one who delivers the opening or greeting remarks.

The selections are meant to honor the two highest-scoring graduates for their efforts. But in recent years, the titles have been construed by some parents as something to give their children an extra advantage in being accepted by a prestigious college or university. Lawsuits have arisen from disputes over who should be tapped for the honors, with school districts caught in between. Some districts have sought to avoid the disputes by naming the top two graduates co-valedictorians. Studies, however, reveal that while quite honorable, the titles do almost nothing to influence which college admission boards.

What should one wear beneath the cap and gown?

It's June and it's hot. Dress lightly, but check with your school officials as to how lightly. Speedos and bikinis might not cut it. Sandals and tennies should be OK, but again check.

After 12 hard years, the kids are ready to party. Where and how?

Many communities throw a "Grad Nite" as a safe and sober celebration. See Chapter 14 for more about Grad Nite.

Doesn't the senior ball come around graduation time?

The senior ball or prom often arrives about the same time as graduation. For more about the prom see Chapter 14.

5

Tests, Report Cards, Homework

From a parent's viewpoint, the most important tests are the ones that directly address your son or daughter's progress in school. Here is a list of these tests followed by explanations:

• **The weekly quizzes** assigned by many teachers. Often these tests are sent home. If you want an immediate "read" on how your child is doing, pay attention to these tests and call the teacher if you spot problems.

• **The STAR test** — two tests given at the same time and treated as one big test. The first part will tell you how your child ranks nationally, the second, how she is doing in mastering the state requirements. See following. STAR is given in the spring with results released usually in August and September. Results are broken out by individual students and by school. The school results are made public, the individual mailed to parents. STAR is given to grades 2 through 11.

For probably most parents, especially up to grade 11, STAR will prove to be the most informative test.

• **Report Card.** Not a test but the summary of the student's work over usually three months. This summary includes the results of tests given in class. This chapter includes a sample report card.

• **College Admission Tests,** the SAT and the ACT. The University of California uses the SAT to help decide admissions and for this reason the SAT is probably more important than the ACT.

These tests are administered by private firms. The PSAT, given in the junior year, has some influence on its own but many students take the test to warm up for the SAT.

• **Exit Exam.** Delayed by arguments for years, this test is supposed to be applied in 2006. Its intent is to prod the low-achieving, especially in high school, into making greater efforts to master the basics. This is a test of the basics.

• **Algebra.** Given for the first time in 2004. Students must pass Algebra I test to graduate from high school.

• **The California English Language Development Test.** Annual test given to immigrant students or students with limited command of English. Its purpose is to determine progress of these students and whether they should be placed in language instruction classes. See Chapter 4, Curriculum.

• **High-school admission tests.** About a half-dozen public high schools in the state determine their admissions by exam. These schools are among the highest scoring in California. Private high schools also may use admission tests.

• **Gifted Screening Test.** Gifted programs break out high-scoring students for special instruction. See Chapter 6, Alternative Education. Schools sometimes use a test to determine admissions to the gifted program. The test is given usually about the third grade.

• **Spot and specialized tests.** As computers and software became more sophisticated, tests were developed to deal with specific situations. One example: Student reads passage, takes short quiz that is fed into classroom computer — instant feedback. Some tests try to identify learning disabilities or areas of reading or math weakness. How these tests are used and what kind are employed vary from school to school.

The STAR Test — Individual Students

Keep in mind that here we are presenting the results as you, the parent, will see them, the results for your son and daughter. The results for the school will have the same categories and additional categories (See pages 97-98, STAR School Results.)

• **National comparison.** Many states have their own tests but it's hard if not impossible to compare results from state to state because the tests or the variables differ.

To get a fix on how students in one state score in relation to students in another state, test developers pulled together a bunch of students that supposedly represented an average American class or school. They gave the kids a certain test and then broke out the results on a bell curve or how the kids scored in relation to one another.

With a bell curve, a small number land at the bottom, a small number at the top, and most about the middle. The scores are ranked by percentiles, 1 (low) to 99 (high). The California Department of Education defines average as a ranking that lands between the 40th and 60th percentile.

This test, part of STAR, is given to California students every year and the results are compared against the rankings from the "representative" group of students. A student who scores in the 90th percentile has done better than 90 percent of other students in the U.S. One who scores in the 10th percentile has landed in the bottom 10 percent of U.S. students.

As might be imagined, this is a crude test but it does give you some idea of where your child stacks up against his national peers.

In grades two to eight, students are tested in reading, language and math. The high-school also tests in these subjects and adds science.

The report you see for your child will list the total questions, the percent correct and the percentile ranking and a bar chart that states: Below average, average, above average.

Very easy to understand.

California Standards Individual Results

The second part of STAR. In grades two to eight, the children are tested in English-Language Arts and General Math. At the high school, they are tested in these subjects and in certain other subjects. If your child takes geometry, for example, he will be tested in geometry.

In the 1990s, California started to put together its standards and assessment programs. (See Chapter 4, Curriculum.) Briefly, the California Department of Education figured out what it wanted the kids to learn at each grade level — the basic curriculum. It then rewrote the textbooks to explain this curriculum and encouraged the districts to teach to the curriculum and standards.

The department also commissioned tests designed specifically for the new curriculum. The California standards results have no connection to the national rankings. Indeed, they are not rankings at all. Neither are they comparisons between students. The results address the question: How well is your child doing in mastering the California basic curriculum?

The "standards" results are presented as Far Below Basic, Below Basic, Basic, Proficient and Advanced.

The results are further detailed as, for example, ninth-grade language arts. This category includes: word analysis and vocabulary, reading comprehension, literary response and analysis, writing conventions and writing strategies. In each subcategory, the individual report will give you the total questions and the percent correct.

This report is also easy to understand.

STAR - School Results, Academic Performance Index

See in this chapter STAR School Results.

College-Admission Tests

The SAT and the ACT. To gain admission to a university, it is not enough to master the basic curriculum. A student must also take more demanding courses and, generally, meet and exceed the A-G requirements of the University of California. See Curriculum, Chapter 4.

Because academic intensity varies by campus, an A grade at one high school cannot be considered the equal of an A grade at another campus. Decades ago, this led to the creation, by private firms, of comprehensive tests — the SAT and the ACT — to identify the top students, no matter what their high-school grades.

In recent years, many people have challenged the validity of these tests but they are still widely used. To meet some of the criticism, the University of California said it would drop the SAT unless it was changed. The test firm agreed; a new SAT is supposed to be fielded in 2006.

So critical are the SAT and the ACT that a thriving industry of test preparers has sprung up to help students get ready for or boost their scores on the SAT and ACT.

Bookstores carry SAT and ACT test preparation books.

The high-school counseling office will also have literature on these tests and when they are given. Also check the admission requirements of the universities.

SAT individual results are released only to the students and to the universities they designate.

SAT results for schools, verbal and math, are released to the public and are often used by parents to assess the academic climate of a high school.

The GED

Or General Educational Development Exam. Many kids bail out of high school, then come to regret not having a diploma. Or they are quitting high school but want some sort of diploma.

Enter the GED (pronounced G-E-D). It's a federal exam and the rough equivalent of a high-school exit exam. If you pass the GED, it tells the world that you have as much basic knowledge as a high-school graduate. The GED can help you secure jobs that require a high-school diploma.

The GED is also given in Spanish and French.

For more information and testing sites, go www.cde.ca.gov/ged.

Social Promotion

For many years, schools and teachers promoted students who just did poorly. Often the children, in knowledge, were several years behind their classmates.

The state now is asking the schools to take a tougher line on social promotion, especially in the early years when repeating a grade might allow a child to catch up.

If your child is having trouble, the teacher should warn you that she might recommend another year in the same grade. You can appeal.

Some people argue that social promotion should be banned, that if a child does not know the material, he should not be advanced.

This is hard to do more than once. Otherwise, the kids would be graduating high school at age 20 or 21 and teenagers would be taking up seats in the seventh grade.

Schools try to keep these youngsters in regular classrooms until high school when they may be enrolled in alternate programs.

STAR - School Results

STAR National Rankings by School

Many parents shopping for homes use the rankings to get a quick read on where a school stacks up academically.

In its annual relocation guides, McCormack's breaks out the rankings for almost all the schools in the metropolitan counties of California along with other school information. www.mccormacks.com. See page 98.

You can also obtain rankings from the state Web site, www.cde.edu and from the individual schools.

In the beginning of this chapter, we described how a representative test is used annually to break out national rankings for individual students.

The same test is used to rank the schools. The numbers run from 1 (low) to 99 (high). The subjects tested are reading, math, language, spelling and at the high school science is added.

A school scoring in the 10th percentile is doing poorly; a school in the 90th percentile is among the top 10 percent in the U.S.

STAR Assessment Rankings By School

This is the counterpart to the STAR assessments by individual students, the one that ranks results by Far Below Basic, Below Basic, Basic, Proficient, Advanced.

This breakout just does it by school. It gives the number of students tested in each subject and percentage that landed in each category, for example

School X. Geometry, 274 tenth graders tested, 32 percent of the tenth grade enrollment.

Level	Percent
Advanced	13%
Proficient	38%
Basic	30%
Below basic	18%

Or the school, in its accountability report card, may provide just the percent scoring above the 50th percentile.

Sample of National Rankings by School

Here's how we present national rankings in McCormack's Relocation guides.

Scores range from 1-99, with 50 the national average. A school scoring 75 has done better than 75 percent of other public schools in the U.S. **Key:** Rd (Reading), Ma (Math), Lg (Language), Sp (Spelling), Sci (Science)

Alameda City Unified School District

Grade	Rd	Ma	Lg	Sp	Sci
Alameda High					
9	51	58	51		54
10	50	66	61		54
11	46	68	54		58
Andersen Comm. Learning					
7	78	74	77	80	
8	60	54	62	66	
9	78	77	87		75
10	71	71	81		66
11	80	83	80		83
Bay Area School					
9	65	50	56		46
10	66	16	51		29
Bay Farm Elem.					
2	81	91	80	84	
3	71	92	76	80	
4	70	78	73	76	
5	80	88	82	82	
6	83	80	84	64	
Chipman Middle					
6	36	37	33	48	
7	36	38	38	44	
8	38	32	37	41	

Grade	Rd	Ma	Lg	Sp	Sci
Earhart Elem.					
2	69	86	75	76	
3	68	76	67	74	
4	70	91	80	83	
5	71	86	75	75	
6	72	77	80	63	
Edison Elem.					
2	86	92	80	80	
3	76	75	71	75	
4	58	60	55	69	
5	71	72	74	58	
Encinal High					
9	53	54	54		45
10	43	40	45		35
11	43	42	45		40
Franklin Elem.					
2	71	83	66	61	
3	61	72	63	67	
4	45	56	47	60	
5	74	63	68	52	
Haight Elem.					
2	46	54	43	59	
3	46	59	40	65	
4	45	56	39	59	
5	39	45	40	53	

Academic Performance Index or API

In the 1980s, a movement surfaced to make public schools "accountable." That is to come up with some system to measure what the kids should be learning and if they weren't coming up to the mark to hold the school and its personnel responsible.

The general thinking at that time was that this could not be done. The conflicts were many and some variables defied measurement — so opponents claimed (and many would still claim).

These conflicts included tests that did not correspond to what was taught in the schools, a curriculum that varied from school to school and textbooks that were out of synch with the curriculum.

The variables included the academic readiness of the children. In certain neighborhoods, parents taught their children the A-B-Cs and got them prepared for kindergarten; in other neighborhoods very little of this happened, in yet others, the kids landed in the middle. This was something the schools had no control over — a major obstacle. If the schools could not control this factor that greatly influenced scores, then, opponents argued, the schools should not be held accountable for the scores.

Further, schools were always changing — through immigration, to economic pressures and home prices, to building patterns. Scores, for reasons explained in Chapter 11, follow demographics.

How Demographics Get Tangled

Here are three common situations in California: a developer builds a middle-class tract in or near a low-income area. Scores in the local school shoot up; nothing has changed at the school except its demographics.

Poor immigrants cluster in certain neighborhoods. Some groups come from countries with good education systems or educational values; others, from countries with failing schools and inattentive academics. One school goes up, one down.

Home prices soar, driving the poor and often the middle class out of some housing markets and into others. In the 1990s, scores shot up in the Central Valley and in parts of Riverside and San Bernardino counties because the middle class was driven inland by home prices in the coastal counties.

In all these situations, the schools were not even players. They educated whomever came through the door.

The Accountability People Win Out

The fight is far from over but in the 1990s in California and about 30 other states accountability, as a movement, caught on.

In California, the accountability proponents, which by this time included many politicians and educators, solved or lessened the conflicts one by one — the tests, the textbooks, the curriculum, teacher training. See Chapter 4 for more on this.

Turning to the variables — migration, immigration, changing demographics, the mix of rich, poor and middle, parental education — they asked the schools to do a much better job of collecting demographic data and they embraced the computer.

Evening Out Boundaries and Demographics

Some school districts, to head off fights, draw attendance boundaries to not only even out enrollments but scores.

Let's take a hypothetical district with 10 elementary schools. Two score high, six about the middle, two low. Down through the years, the district will probably get many requests to transfer to the two highest schools.

One way to deal with this: Change the demographics of two top schools by placing within their attendance zones neighborhoods with low or middling demographics.

Result: Scores come up slightly in the other schools and go down slightly in the two highest schools. Fewer requests for transfers. The downside: The district might go through holy hell changing the attendance borders.

Another occasional scenario: Old town with old high school adds new tracts and has to build a second high school. The money comes from fees leveled on the new buyers. Up goes the school and it's a beauty, everything state-of-the-art.

But the district doesn't make sweeping changes in its attendance zones. Many kids from the new tracts are still assigned to the old high school, which compared to the new, is a mangy old mutt. New parents say, hey, I am being taxed for the new school but my kids are not allowed to attend it. Grumble, grumble.

Parents in old town, whose kids still attend old high school, also start muttering. The new school is so much better than the old. This is not fair. Grumble, grumble.

From such passions, school bonds are proposed and passed. The bond raises money to renovate or rebuild the old school.

None of this would have come to pass without advances in computers and software. The new technology allowed the department of education to collect and analyze data and turn out reports very quickly.

The data collected on individual students includes information on family income, ethnic group, native or immigrant and command of English. Some of the information comes from forms parents fill out; some indirectly. Family income is determined in part by applications for subsidized lunches.

Moving To Measure

With these changes and new tools, the bureaucrats became confident that they could do what before was impossible: factor out the variables (demographics) and come up with a measuring system that could identify where breakdowns were occurring. Once the breakdowns were identified, schools would be expected to make corrections.

Big task. Complex. Still incomplete, still bugs to be ironed out. Changes are being made from year to year.

In California, the department of education, for schools, not individual students, devised a system that ranged from 200 to 1,000 with "proficiency" defined as a score of 800. Every school was tested and given a baseline according to test results.

Let's look at a school that scored 400, low. At this point, the state would say OK, you scored low. That doesn't bother us. But we want you to improve next year. We don't expect you to hit 800 but how about notching up your score by about 5 percent. This notching up is called a "target." We want you to hit your target next year.

The school might reply, well, wait a second, we just got a big influx of low-scoring, low-income kids. You can't expect us to boost our scores.

The state would say, you're right. This is unfair. But we're going to take this into account when we configure your next baseline.

Which is what the state does every year. It starts each school off with a new baseline and target, working in demographic data and changes in tests and other changes. (With demographic shifts, the scores might not be reported for a year.)

Instead of starting at 400, this school might be given a baseline on 390 and a target of 411 or if the demographics went upscale, a baseline of 430 and a target of 459. This baseline and target and goal setting was given the collective name of the Academic Performance Index or API.

This may confuse many people because school progress has never been presented this way.

You don't say to your kid, "OK Johnny, we moved last year and you're in a new school. I'm going to allow for confusion and adjust our expectations. Last year, you were getting As and Bs; let's start with Cs and see if you can work your way up."

Or something like that. We're used to starting at a fixed point and trying to move up.

Academic Performance Index — Simplified

In one of its plainest presentations, the Academic Performance Index (API) might look like this:

School X

Percent tested: 97

API Base: 703

Growth Target: 5 (state wants school to go up five points to 708)

Growth Score: 718 (School actually goes up 15 points; well done!)

School Y

Percent tested: 96

API Base: 656

Growth target: 3 (state has set benchmark of 659)

Growth Score: 646 (Instead of going up, school drops 10 points; has not hit its target).

Information Galore

The Academic Performance Index breaks out scores by other categories:

• State Rank. On a scale of 1 to 10, by API score, each school is ranked against all other schools in the state. One is low, ten high.

• Rank by comparable school. The state compiles the demographics of School X then compares its score to the scores of 100 other schools with similar demographics. This ranking is also 1 to 10.

• Results by ethnicity and socioeconomics.

The Academic Performance Index is usually released at the beginning of the calendar year. It is not mailed to parents but much of it is included in the School Accountability Report Cards (SARC). Many newspapers will carry the index.

Other reports break out results by male and female, parent education, disability and English proficiency.

In the 1990s, parents and schools were starved for information about schools and scores. Now there are loads of data out there; much is easily understood and easily accessed through the California Department. of Education Web site, www.cde.gov.

Fun Ahead

California and the federal government are arguing over what to do with this information. See No Child Left Behind in Chapter 4.

In a nutshell, the state wants to take the data and gently push the schools and school districts into higher scores.

The feds want to kick the schools into higher scores and if they can't hit their targets, close them or change their staffs.

What Do You Want To Do?

You're the parent. You don't have to play by the same rules as the state and the feds. You can, for example, use the data to get some idea of how fast the school is pacing itself and how well the teacher is doing his job. A lot of this will be looking through the glass darkly but a murky look is better than flying blind.

One of the uncomfortable truths about schools is that they can't accomplish everything. They never could. They are run by human beings. They are often hemmed in by regulations. They have their conflicts, which are not going away and which sometimes play out to the disadvantage of some of the students.

The active parent often has to be the savvy parent who makes up some of the deficiencies of the schools or intervenes when certain choices have to be made. The more information you have, the better, possibly, your decisions will be. See Chapter 6, Scores.

Report Cards

Report cards come from the teacher. Although they follow a set format, they really are informal assessments on how well your child is doing within the class.

One of their main purposes is to alert you (the parent) to problems and enlist your support in solving or lessening them.

Report cards typically divide into manners and work habits and academic problems and pluses. They give the teacher an opportunity to rate your child on such skills as following rules, respecting others and working diligently.

On the academic side, the teacher will rate your child on such subjects as math, reading and writing.

In recent years, as part of the curriculum overhaul, schools have been correlating the academic categories with the material in the curriculum and using the new language of standards and assessments.

The old-style report cards, which are still used widely, gave students a letter grade, A, B, C, D, F, for their academic efforts, A being the highest mark.

The new-style cards might use something like:

1. Experiencing difficulty at grade-level standard.

2. Approaching grade-level standard.

3. Proficient or benchmark at grade-level standard.

If your child is having trouble, the school will probably ask you to come in for talk about What To Do.

Even if your child is not having problems, you might want to use the occasion to check with the teacher about your child's progress or get answers to any questions you might have. Or just to get to know the teacher.

Report cards are mailed to parents at the midpoint of every term or semester and at the end.

If you don't get one, it may have been intercepted by you-know-who, your heir or heiress. Check with the school.

Sample Report Card

Here is a report card, slightly altered, used by a mid-sized California district. Instead of concentrating on one grade, the report card draws from several grade levels to give an idea of what is being rated.

Lifelong Learning Skills

Skills are rated:

E: Excellent
S: Satisfactory
N: Needs Improvement

Social Skills

- Shows respect for peers
- Shows respect for adults
- Shows respect for property
- Shows respect for learning
- Follows classroom rules
- Follows playground rules
- Follows school rules
- Accepts responsibility for own actions
- Chooses appropriate strategies to resolve conflict

Work Habits

- Works independently
- Works cooperatively
- Listens to and follows directions
- Uses time effectively
- Is developing organizational skills
- Exhibits neat and legible work
- Contributes appropriately to class activities
- Uses school materials responsibly
- Completes classwork carefully and on time
- Completes homework carefully and on time

Sample Report Card (Cont.)

Mathematical Reasoning
- Understands and uses appropriate math vocabulary
- Uses estimation skills to verify the reasonableness of answers
- Applies strategies, skills, and concepts from simpler problems in finding solutions to complex problems
- Uses pictures, models, graphs and charts to solve problems

Numbers
- Counts, reads and writes numbers to 10,000
- Compares and orders numbers to 10,000
- Memorizes multiplication tables for numbers from 0 to 10
- Adds and subtracts whole numbers up to 10,000
- Multiplies and divides multi-digit numbers by one-digit numbers
- Compares, adds, and subtracts simple fractions
- Uses expanded notation to represent numbers

Algebra and Fractions
- Represents relationships of quantities using expressions, equations, inequalities
- Solves simple problems involving the relationship between two quantities (e.g., find the total cost of multiple items given the cost per unit)

Measurement and Geometry
- Finds the perimeter and estimates area of shapes
- Identifies the attributes of triangles and quadrilaterals
- Chooses appropriate units/tools and measures length, area, liquid, volume, and weight

Statistics, Data, Analysis and Probability
- Identifies whether common events are certain, likely, unlikely or improbable
- Records, displays, and summarizes results from simple probability experiments

Sample Report Card (Cont.)

Reading
- Decodes multisyllabic words (three or more syllables)
- Reads grade-level narrative and expository texts with fluency and expression
- Uses knowledge of prefixes and suffixes to determine the meaning of words
- Uses knowledge of word families to decode unfamiliar words
- Uses knowledge of antonyms, synonyms & homophones to determine word meaning
- Understands grade-level text using a variety of comprehension strategies
- Distinguishes main idea and supporting details
- Interprets and applies meaning to text (problems and solutions)
- Follows simple multiple-step written instructions
- Distinguishes common forms of literature (poetry, drama, fiction, nonfiction)

Writing
- Writes a paragraph with a topic sentence, supporting details and a conclusion
- Uses the writing process for narratives and descriptions
- Writes personal and formal letters
- Uses correct sentence structure
- Uses correct capitalization, punctuation, and grammar
- Uses correct grade-level spelling in written work
- Writes legibly in cursive with correct form

Speaking and Listening
- Engages in coherent, descriptive, well organized oral communication
- Retells, paraphrases, and explains what has been said by speaker
- Tells a story with a beginning, middle, and end

Gathering Information
- Uses a variety of reference materials to collect, organize and present information

How Good Are Our Top Schools

For over 20 years, McCormack's has published relocation-newcomer guides to the metropolitan counties of California. See www.mccormacks.com. These books include school rankings and three or four times a year someone will ask us, how good are the top California schools versus the top East Coast schools. This question also shows up in the media.

We tell them that accurate comparisons are impossible but our guess is that our tops are as good as their tops and we advise them to look at the national percentile rankings and at the SAT scores by state.

Page 98 illustrates how we present the percentile rankings. Pages 110-111 shows a recent breakout of SAT scores by state.

The percentile rankings would seem to be a good indicator because they are based on a test of students who supposedly represent an average American school. (See pages 93 and 94.) But California schools are not "representative." We have far more limited-English-speaking students than almost any other state. Further, many of our top schools are neighborhood schools that include many middle and middle-plus scoring students.

If you go by the math SAT, the smartest students in the nation can be found in North Dakota, 610 and in Iowa, 602 — as opposed to California's 517. But only 4 percent of North Dakota's seniors take the SAT and only 5 percent of Iowa's. On the other hand, 52 percent of California's seniors take the SAT.

The SAT scores for such states as Massachusetts, Vermont, New Hampshire and Maine would seem to indicate that they do a better job — high percentage of test takers, scores close to California — but these states may not be as diverse and may not have as many limited-English, as California. New York, a diverse state, has many limited-English and a higher number of SAT testers but its SAT scores are slightly lower than California's.

A state that has many universities (Massachusetts) also will have many academic families that typically score high. The scores may reflect the background of the kids and not the quality of the schools.

From percentiles and the SAT scores, you can get the big picture; it's the detailed comparison that's the problem.

The same with international comparisons. They should not be ignored because they may indicate genuine failings but they also need context. Several years ago, California elementary schools were blasted for low scores in science. A problem ... yes. But possibly not because the kids were failing science; rather, the schools were failing to teach them science in the K-8 system. If the kids were tested in high school, where science is taught, they might have made a better showing.

At least one educational theory excuses all our shortcomings. It holds that many Asian and European students work hard in the K-12 grades because this decides if they will get into a quality university. When they reach the university, they kick back; there is very little academic pressure. On the U.S. side, even marginal students attend universities but unless they buckle down, they get forced out. Or they go into the work force from high school, see how much a degree is valued, then return to school older and wiser (and harder working) and get the sheepskin.

With this theory, by the age of 30, our students are as smart or as ignorant as their foreign counterparts.

Academic Decathlon

The Academic Decathlon is a statewide series of regional competitions that culminate in one statewide championship, the winner of which competes in the national. Open to any public or private school, it features high-school students competing in academic events including: art economics, language, literature, math, music, science and social science. Additionally, each team member makes both a prepared and impromptu speech, submits to an interview and writes an essay. The Super Quiz, which focused on the Lewis and Clark expedition in the 2003-2004 national decathlon, is the Decathlon's 10th event.

On a local level, schools often host science fairs where students are challenged to tackle a scientific question and answer it using the scientific method. Some projects can get very elaborate with robots, computers and pictorial displays. Topics can range from complex physiological issues to various weather issues. Some can be rather whimsical. One youngster tackled the aromatic question of "Why my feet stink." More than testing students' talents in science, the fairs are an exercise in critical thinking and problem-solving.

National Scholastic Aptitude Test (SAT) Scores

State	*Tested (%)	Verbal	Math
Alabama	9	560	559
Alaska	52	516	519
Arizona	36	520	523
Arkansas	5	560	556
California	52	496	517
Colorado	28	543	548
Connecticut	83	509	509
Delaware	69	502	500
Dist. of Columbia	76	480	473
Florida	57	496	499
Georgia	65	489	491
Hawaii	53	488	520
Idaho	18	539	541
Illinois	11	578	596
Indiana	62	498	503
Iowa	5	591	602
Kansas	9	578	580
Kentucky	12	550	552
Louisiana	8	561	559
Maine	69	503	502
Maryland	67	507	513
Massachusetts	81	512	516
Michigan	11	558	572
Minnesota	10	581	591
Mississippi	4	559	547
Missouri	8	574	580
Montana	23	541	547
Nebraska	8	561	570
Nevada	34	509	518
New Hampshire	73	519	519
New Jersey	82	498	513
New Mexico	14	551	543
New York	79	494	506
North Carolina	67	493	505
North Dakota	4	597	610
Ohio	27	533	540
Oklahoma	8	565	562

Oregon	56	524	528
Pennsylvania	72	498	500
Rhode Island	73	504	503
South Carolina	59	488	493
South Dakota	5	576	586
Tennessee	14	562	555
Texas	55	491	500
Utah	6	563	559
Vermont	69	512	510
Virginia	68	510	506
Washington	54	525	529
West Virginia	18	525	515
Wisconsin	7	583	599
Wyoming	11	531	537
Nationwide	**46**	**504**	**516**

Source: California Dept. of Education, 2002 tests.
*Percentage of class taking the test.

Homework

After parents for years complained that their children were getting too much homework, one of the national think tanks, Brookings Institution, studied the matter. Its conclusion, released in 2003:

Teachers today are demanding as much homework as teachers 50 years ago.

Only one age group showed an increase: Children ages 6 to 8. Between 1981, their homework increased from 52 minutes a week to 128 minutes, up 146 percent.

This sounds like an awful lot but the details present a much different picture.

When the study started, many children in this age group were not doing any homework at all.

Now, with the emphasis on improving the early grades, more children age 6-8 are doing at least a little homework, and this simple change accounted for most of the 146 percent.

How much homework should you expect for your children? Here's a rough guide from a news article:

For every year, add 10 minutes a night. That is 30 minutes for a third grader, 80 for an eighth grader and two hours for a high-school senior.

In our research we came across articles on high-school students who were doing up to three hours a night in the hope of getting accepted by a tough university. This seemed to suggest that the highly ambitious should be swotting up to the three-hour mark.

But in 2002, UCLA released a survey of 282,000 college freshmen and only 34 percent said they spent more than an hour a weekday on homework during their senior year.

Who is doing their homework? One news article said that "international studies show" — delightfully vague — that the French, the Russians, the Italians and the South Africans spend twice as much time at homework than our students.

Probably true but it may not be advisable to tell your darlings that their grades would be much higher if only they followed the example of, the French, etc. Foreign relations are rocky enough as it is.

Here some advice from educators on ways to make homework easier and less argumentive:

• Determine the setting. If Johnny works better alone, if Maria prefers the kitchen table, decide the location and stick with it.

• Keep reference materials, such as a dictionary, in a convenient place. Also paper and pens.

• Nail down a time when the homework is to be done.

• Keep on the kids while they work. You don't have to hover; just let them know that Mom or Pop has an open eye.

• Turn off the television or radio. Create quiet.

• One educator swore by this tactic: take a calendar and help your kid create a schedule of homework and activities. Many teachers hand out the weekly assignments on Monday; this would help in setting up a calendar.

• Encourage the lad or lass to join a homework club, if the school has one.

• Many teachers now post the homework assignment on a Web site or voice mail. If yours doesn't, ask her to. Some teachers hand out sheets. Get the sheet.

• At the beginning of the school year talk to the teacher and find out how she assigns homework and if she has penalties and rewards.

• Avoid doing your kid's homework. Try to teach the skills that will get the job done. If the student has a question about directions or some aspect of the assignment, be helpful but not over-helpful.

• Do you have: no patience, an uncontrollable desire to watch The Sopranos or any cop show, a job that leaves you exhausted, no temperament for setting homework rules? But you have money. Hire a tutor. If you don't have money, do your best, try for the homework club and talk to the teacher.

• If your child is trying hard and putting in the time but can't get the assignment done, talk to the teacher. There might be a learning problem.

6

What Scores Mean
Why Rich Towns Score High
Low & Middle-Scoring Schools:
Can They Do the Job?

- **• TENSIONS AND DISPUTES**
- **• SOCIOECONOMICS**
- **• ACHIEVEMENT**
- **• PACING**

Socioeconomics

If you delve beneath the surface of schools, you will inevitably come across socioeconomics.

Down through the years and especially with the introduction of computers, social scientists and such groups as the California Department of Education have been collecting data on students and correlating it with school scores.

They have found that family income and parents' education strongly correlate with school scores. To put it crudely, which is how it often winds up in the media, the richer you are, the more you are educated, the higher your kid will score.

From this, some people conclude that ... Wow! Here's the real reason why the wealthy score high. They spend more money on education, they hire tutors, take trips abroad and send their kids to enriched classes. Being educated, they know how to work the system.

The authors of this book have sent their kids through California schools and as reporters and researchers have talked to many teachers, visited a variety of schools and attended hundreds of school-board meetings.

We agree that money counts! It can help buy your child if not a good education at least a better one.

Mom and pop's education counts. If you know how the schools work, you will often have an edge over parents who don't.

The socioeconomic index can be uncannily and depressingly accurate. So accurate in fact that it makes education seem like a numbers game: No matter what schools do, family background and income determines almost all.

But There Are A Few Jokers In The Deck

They go by a variety of names: values, culture, the push from home, the neighborhood and school environment, school quality, the influence of the kids' friends, the ideas and temper of the times. Some contradictions:

This country is full of groups that arrived almost penniless, had little or no education in the old country and yet raised children who went on to secure university degrees and move up the ladder. We still have them. We still have social mobility— not perhaps as much we should, but it's there.

California and the nation have a fair number of communities that score above their economic weight. They include Cerritos, Albany, Davis and, at the middle level many of the rural-suburban communities of the Central Valley and such places as Riverside and San Bernardino counties.

We also have in this country some groups that score below their economic status.

Lastly, we have in the U.S. over 40 years of experimentation with the schools and a great variety of social-educational models, including some that have pumped a great deal of money into low-income, low-scoring schools. The results: There are a few models that seem encouraging, including some in California.

But in many instances, the money has not elevated academics or scores or raised them just a little. To cite just one example, Washington D.C. spends over twice as much per student as California and yet its scores are low. (This is not an argument for skimping on funding.)

What's going on? Let's start with the question:

Why Do Kids In Rich Neighborhoods Score High

Some preliminaries: You can be well educated in the U.S. and not be rich. Many people fall into this category.

But generally if you're rich, you are well educated. Which is only to say that to rise in business and government, to secure the better jobs and promotions in our modern, complex society, you pretty much have to have a college degree.

Affluent people often group together. In many instances, the clusters are quite clear: communities that are almost completely affluent — Piedmont, Saratoga, Arcadia, Beverly Hills, Rancho Santa Fe, Orinda, Tiburon, etc.

Sometimes the divisions are muddled. Many cities mix rich, poor and middle but break them out in distinct neighborhoods. Los Angeles — South Central, poor; Bel Air, rich; San Diego — Logan Heights, poor; La Jolla, rich; San Francisco — Bayview-Hunters Point, poor; Pacific Heights, rich, and so on.

Without getting bogged down in details, one of the big dividers is home price. As a rule — but with interesting exceptions — the higher the price, the higher the scores.

Rich kids are not always brilliant kids. Many score just above or just below the 50th percentile — average. Here's a common pattern in California, taken from actual scores.

School A. Located in an affluent neighborhood. All students are from the neighborhood. Overall scores in the 95th percentile, top 5 percent in the state.

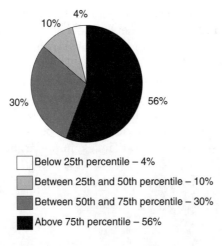

4%

10%

30%

56%

Below 25th percentile – 4%

Between 25th and 50th percentile – 10%

Between 50th and 75th percentile – 30%

Above 75th percentile – 56%

School B. Scores in the 80th percentile, top 20 percent in the state.

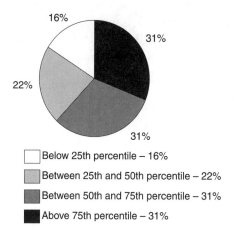

16%

31%

22%

31%

☐ Below 25th percentile – 16%

▨ Between 25th and 50th percentile – 22%

▨ Between 50th and 75th percentile – 31%

■ Above 75th percentile – 31%

Prepared

But if not brilliant, many students at the top-scoring schools are prepared.

They enter kindergarten or the first-grade knowing the alphabet or even reading. They may even know how to write simple sentences. They probably will have some social skills that help academically — sitting still, keeping quiet when told, and so on.

And when this happens, good things follow at the school.

The Bonuses

Parents breathing down their necks, the kids are less likely to get into trouble, to drain the staff's energy on discipline — which at many low-scoring schools is a big problem.

The students are more likely to do their homework, to come to school ready to work. This allows the class to move at a good pace and the teacher to hand out more homework. With so many kids scoring high, it's often easy to find enough kids to fill advanced classes. Discussions may be livelier, distractions fewer.

At recess and in the playground and after school, the kids hang around with kids who read books and maybe have some polished social skills. These days, etiquette classes are showing up in the affluent towns. Back-to-school nights are crowded with parents. Teachers get a lot of stroking, a lot of attention.

Other Forces At Work

Parents with sophisticated skills may volunteer their talents in class projects that benefit students generally. In Silicon Valley, parents help set up computer classes and advise schools on computer and software purchases. At one school, a parent, a lawyer, advised the debating team. Beverly Hills High School is famous for its performing arts program, which is strongly supported by parents and the town.

Sometimes little things count in a big way. The pupils are asked to write essays, which are posted on the wall. Naturally, the kids write about themselves and their families. My dad is a lawyer, my mom is a manager. Success permeates the school.

What About Teacher Quality And Programs?

You can have attentive kids and supportive parents but if the teachers are ignorant and the programs faulty, the students might not learn much of value.

The high-scoring schools often do not pay the top wages but they generally have little trouble attracting credentialed teachers. The same for many middle-scoring schools. The schools that have the hiring difficulties are located in inner cities and even these schools often will have competent teachers. (See Chapter 3, Teachers.)

The difference at the high-scoring school comes down to the ways the teachers interact with parents and the school. If Johnny is having a problem, mom or dad is usually on the phone right away. Or at the school.

Years ago, a group of Berkeley parents seeking to raise scores at their schools tried to identify the characteristics of "high-scoring" parents, namely themselves. One conclusion: They nagged the teachers and school administrators a lot. The logical next step, a la Berkeley, which fortunately was not taken, classes on how to nag.

But you get the point: The parents are not only breathing down the backs of the kids, they are also huffing and puffing over the teacher and, many times, trying to help her with her job. They are engaged. If a principal makes a bad hire, the parents are going to let her know. If the teacher is new and on probation, she might not be hired permanently.

It should be noted, however, that some effective parents, drawing on different cultural experiences, are not actively connected with the schools. They send their kids to school with strict orders to behave and obey the teachers. And they make sure the homework gets done. Seems to work.

Programs And Extracurricular Activities

The same programs taught in other California schools will be taught in the high-performance schools. At the high school, college-prep courses will be emphasized because many of the students are college bound.

But what takes students at other schools months to master may be absorbed in weeks by the high-scoring group. This will allow the teacher to move deeper into the curriculum or to introduce other subjects or present an enriched program.

The school's program, in large part, is defined by the abilities of the students.

The low-scoring schools often spend a lot of time on the basics. (See Chapter 4, Curriculum.) The high-scoring schools will move faster through the basics and create time for science or art or music.

If there is a problem with a program, if it is not working the way it should, parents often will speak up. They pay attention to the little things, especially in university neighborhoods where parents are almost fanatical on school matters.

High-performance schools have many clubs. To sample just one school in the San Francisco area: art, baking, beading, black student union, chess, Christian, debate, environmental, feminist, fishing, frisbee, math, gay-straight, guitar, history, movie, model United Nations, Junior Statesmen, Latino, photo, roller hockey, singing, literary magazine, French, Spanish, Italian and about 10 more. This high school, located next to a university, is unusually bountiful in its club choices.

In 2002, the Sacramento Bee surveyed 52 public high schools to assess how they differed in club activities. The newspaper's finding: Big campuses and middle income and affluent campuses did a better job than small campuses and campuses with many low-income children.

Many of the clubs and activities owed their existence to parental vigor, sometimes coming in surprising ways, for instance, the amount of money raised by sports booster clubs.

Enter The Dollar

If a child at a high-scoring school is falling behind and the school for whatever reason can't correct the problem, parents often resort to tutors.

We know of one situation where parents thought a particular high-school teacher was incompetent. The person had tenure; there was no way to get rid of her. The parents chipped in, hired a tutor off campus, and created a shadow class that went over the material the teacher botched. Money at work but also knowledge — the parents knew how to get around the problems of the system.

Affluent parents routinely pay for cramming classes to help raise scores on college-admission tests (SAT, ACT).

Almost all high-scoring schools have active parents' clubs. They raise hundreds of thousands and sometimes over $1 million for their schools.

Some affluent districts pass parcel taxes, which require two-thirds approval, hard to get. The money is used to maintain and improve academic programs and electives, such as band.

If you buy into the money argument — schools succeed, fail or stumble along according to their funding you will always have ammunition to support your position. Money does make a difference.

But the money argument ...

Carries only so much weight. Many high-scoring districts receive proportionally less money from the state than lower-scoring districts. (See Chapter 10, Finance.)

As for the parcel taxes, yes, some districts pass them but not that many. Almost all these districts are located in Northern California. Southern Cal really is as anti-tax as it is made out to be. But many Southern California schools score high.

In many instances, the money raised by parents is not that great, $250 to $500 per child.

The real benefit may come in how it is spent. For legal reasons, the money is controlled by the parents' clubs and these clubs have many parents volunteering in the schools. They see firsthand what the school lacks and they often fund these needs. If they gave the money with no strings attached to the school or district, it might go for institutional priorities, such as maintenance and salaries, not academic tasks.

The Values Factor

The richest neighborhoods don't always have the highest scoring schools.

Three exceptions: Albany district in the San Francisco area, Davis district in Central California and Cerritos schools in the ABC district in Los Angeles County.

Albany was built for blue-collar workers; the great majority of the homes are old and small, two and three bedrooms.

Davis is middle class. Tract housing, three and four bedrooms, well maintained, but very little jumping up the scale.

Both districts are high scoring and have high schools that top the 600 mark in the math SAT, something achieved annually in California by only about two dozen schools.

Both are university towns, Albany for UC Berkeley, Davis for UC Davis, and illustrate the values argument. Many of the parents probably earn good money but are not rich. They are college grads and soaked in academics and have high ambitions for their children.

Cerritos in the ABC district has a more interesting situation. It is not a university town. In per capita income, according to the 2000 census, Cerritos ranked 40th among Los Angeles County's 125 communities. Its housing runs to upper-middle tracts, many four bedrooms, presentable but not overwhelming.

Boundary Fights

School districts often have to change attendance boundaries. Old neighborhoods that used to have many young families now have few; new neighborhoods often bring in young families. Some schools may be overflowing with students, others may have empty seats.

The changes sometimes blossom into major disputes. Parents may have an emotional attachment to a certain school or find it convenient to their home.

Other times, they object because the changes will affect the school's demographics and, sometimes, its programs. And maybe the neighborhood's property values.

If a neighborhood with schools scoring in the 90s couples with a neighborhood with scores in the 50s, the overall scores will probably go down. Moreover, the school may have to drop some of its high-end programs and move toward general education.

The ABC district has many low-scoring schools. The district takes in all or parts of four cities: One city scores low, one scores generally low-middle, the third middle-high, and Cerritos, among the tops in the state.

Without taking anything away from the schools and their teachers, Cerritos has many students of Asian descent, a group famous for its educational values. How they came by these values is beyond the scope of this book.

Money! Yes important, but values, also very important. By values, we mean the time and energy you put into your child's education, the attention you pay, the efforts you make, the neighborhood setting. These things can take a variety of forms.

The Problems At Top Schools

Some kids will get into trouble with drugs and sex. Some will drop out or get low grades.

Not all the teachers will be top notch. Many students go on to community colleges and state universities— certainly respectable choices but not the top universities.

The helpful parent, in reality, may be an interfering, overbearing parent.

The school's teachers may not be able to afford the town and this might wear on staff morale.

Many high-scoring schools are not ethnically or socially diverse. The students may turn out clever but possibly not wise; they have not been exposed to the problems of the greater society.

But by and large, these schools are considered successes. And the market recognizes them as successes. When you buy a home in a high-scoring district, it is generally recognized that the good schools have boosted the price.

Why, Precisely, Is The Rich School A Success?

It's hard to say because the elements blend into and nourish one another.

The kids came prepared. The parents pushed and funded and put in a lot of time and energy. Teachers were able to move quickly through the curriculum, the extracurricular choices were plentiful and the program was enriched.

What we can say for certain is that schools and neighborhoods and parents, and the ways they interact, greatly determine how the education of the children turns out.

When you look at the scores, you're not just getting a snapshot of the school. You're getting a report, somewhat obscure and contradictory, on the values, academic intensity, personality, history and culture of the family and neighborhood. And often the school will shape itself to the realities of the family and neighborhood. Here we get into one of the trickiest parts of education.

Good School — Low Scores

A "good" school can have low scores. By good, we mean a well-trained, hard-working staff. Clever and well-conceived programs. Good discipline and effective use of time. The state and federal departments of education explicitly recognize this in their assessment programs. They don't take the schools to task for low scores; they get on them when they fail to improve these scores.

Schools take the children as they come through the door. If the children are unprepared, if they have weak or little support at home or in the neighborhood, for whatever reason, that's the reality the school has to live with and adjust to. Often this means

Low Scores but Pat On the Back

In 1999, California came up with an example that illustrates some of the difficulties of assessing schools.

Sheppard Elementary School, located near Santa Rosa, won a national Blue Ribbon for its programs and the quality of its instruction. At the same time, Sheppard was placed on the list of underperforming schools and told to shape up.

The Blue Ribbon came from the U.S. Department of Education; the censure came from the California Department of Education. Each was working off a different set of expectations.

Sheppard had many students who spoke little English. Nine of every ten of its students came from low-income families.

Delaine Eastin, at that time the California Superintendent of Public Instruction, presented the Blue Ribbon and said that because of socioeconomic factors, schools such as Sheppard could do an exceptional job but still turn out low-achieving students.

that the school, no matter how accomplished the staff, has to concentrate on the basics and on rudimentary instruction. For this reason, the program and the pacing at a low-scoring school often will be much different than the one at the high scoring school.

At this point you might be thinking ...

Life Is Not Fair

No kidding! You're ambitious for your child. You're willing to put in the time on homework and on reading and getting the kid ready for school. You show up for teacher conferences and, in short, do as much as your job, energy and time permit to advance your child's education. But with homes priced about two miles above the wild blue yonder you can't afford to buy into a high-performance, affluent community.

You live in — and you can fill in your own blank — a neighborhood where scores are low or middling. Is there any hope for your child?

Yes! Schools also acknowledge the complexity of mixed demographics and the necessity for different programs. But many arguments and tensions come into play. You have to be aware of programs and pacing. Let's look at these examples, drawn from California schools.

Overall Scores Low To Middling; Achievement High

This pattern shows up in the districts that mix high and low-scoring kids. El Cerrito High and Berkeley High in the San Francisco area are good examples. These schools are located near UC Berkeley and attract students from the academic community. At the same time, they draw many students from low-income neighborhoods and low-scoring schools.

The overall academic rankings of these schools, based on STAR tests, is about the 50th percentile, middling.

Nonetheless, both these schools every year advance many students to the University of California and top universities and are believed to have solid prep programs. These schools also run programs for the lower-scoring students. As the scores indicate, many of these programs are basic and remedial.

The schools have adjusted to the realities of their communities.

There's a fair number of schools like this throughout California, some of them located in such affluent counties as Santa Barbara, San Mateo and Marin.

Berkeley High

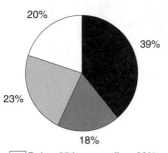

20%

39%

23%

18%

☐ Below 25th percentile – 20%

▨ Between 25th and 50th percentile – 23%

▨ Between 50th and 75th percentile – 18%

■ Above 75th percentile – 39%

El Cerrito High

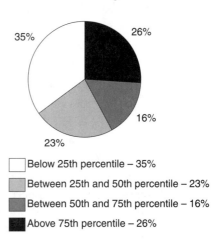

35%

26%

16%

23%

☐ Below 25th percentile – 35%

▨ Between 25th and 50th percentile – 23%

▨ Between 50th and 75th percentile – 16%

■ Above 75th percentile – 26%

School districts often include very diverse neighborhoods. Rich and poor kids find themselves in the same school. The school devises programs according to academic prowess of the children.

So to answer the question, can your child succeed at a school with overall scores low to middling, the answer is, many students at these school do quite well.

But, read on; it's not as easy at these examples might suggest. Quite the opposite.

The Middle-Scoring School

Drawing on actual schools, here's a roughly representative example of how a middle-scoring school, 50th and 60th percentile in state rankings, breaks out academically.

Rounded school, middle America. Many parents like these schools because many children score in the middle and are comfortable in these schools.

These schools will have programs for low, middle and high achievers.

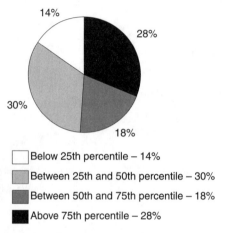

14%

28%

30%

18%

☐ Below 25th percentile – 14%

▨ Between 25th and 50th percentile – 30%

▧ Between 50th and 75th percentile – 18%

■ Above 75th percentile – 28%

If 15 percent of the first grade can't read, the teacher can devote 15 percent of her time or even more to these students and still have enough time for the other students.

The high school will have its nerds and its jocks and its newspaper. Back-to-school and Open House will draw many parents. Teacher quality is apt to be good because this type school will draw many applicants for the teaching slots. Many of the teachers will live locally; the town's housing will be affordable.

The drawbacks: Academic intensity probably will not be as great as what's found in the high-scoring schools. Or at schools such as Berkeley High or El Cerrito High.

In an average year, the "average" high school might advance 9 percent of its seniors to a University of California, which, with exceptions, takes the top 12.5 percent. By comparison, a high-performance school will advance about 20 percent of its students to a UC. When you add in the students who attend a top private university or a good out-of-state college, the percentage attending elite institutions rises.

The Low-Middle School

A school scoring about the 30th percentile will show approximately:

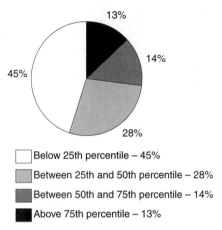

Below 25th percentile – 45%
Between 25th and 50th percentile – 28%
Between 50th and 75th percentile – 14%
Above 75th percentile – 13%

Put yourself in the place of the principal of this school. About 73 percent of your students are scoring under the 50th percentile. Where are you going to put your energy and resources? Probably toward remedial, toward basic instruction.

But you also have a fair number of students about mid range and a small group scoring higher? Some schools might install an internal "academy" and break out the higher achieving in their own classes. It might have different programs for each group.

Scholastic intensity? Hard to say. A well-managed school might do a good job.

Admissions to a UC — 5 to 7 percent of the senior class.

Very low

A school in the 10th to 20th percentiles might show this pattern:

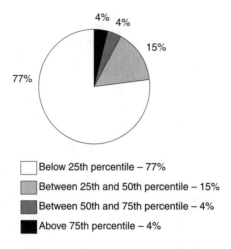

4% 4%

15%

77%

☐ Below 25th percentile – 77%

▨ Between 25th and 50th percentile – 15%

▨ Between 50th and 75th percentile – 4%

■ Above 75th percentile – 4%

Have to go slow. Many kids need a lot of work on basics. Note the small number of high scoring. Almost every school, no matter where it's located, will have at least a few kids who score high or fairly high.

If there is enough of them, the school might break them out in their own classes or cluster them for several hours a week.

Also, the principal and the staff might find ways to keep the students engaged.

The movies sometimes show teachers as blockheads, unable to spot talent even when it is staring them in the face. Or in some ways unappreciative of talent.

Anything is possible but this scenario is highly unlikely. Teachers work with the kids day in and out. They get to know them well. Teachers generally enjoy kids who are achieving. These kids make the school look good. They bump up the test results.

To bring in diversity, the UC's are accepting the top 4 percent of each high school (but certain requirements have to be met).

Changing Schools, Rural Mixed With Suburban

Many parts of the San Francisco Bay Area and of Los Angeles, Orange and San Diego counties have priced young families out of the housing market. Often these parents are college educated and middle class.

To serve this group, developers are moving way inland, where land prices and building costs are cheaper, and erecting large tracts in what used to be farming villages or blue-collar towns.

Rural areas have many immigrant and migrant workers; scores are very low. In comes a developer, up goes a tract. Not a rich tract; often the homes sell for $200,000 to $300,000. Nonetheless, the change is striking. Schools that were scoring in the 10th percentiles jump to 40th and 50th.

This school might show this kind of pattern, taken from a Central Valley farm town that recently built suburban tracts.

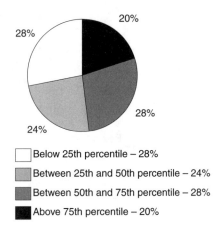

Below 25th percentile – 28%
Between 25th and 50th percentile – 24%
Between 50th and 75th percentile – 28%
Above 75th percentile – 20%

Or the new tract builds its own school, which serves the immediate neighborhood. Scores land above the 50th percentile. A mile so away in the same district is the old school, scores 10th to 20th percentile.

If what happens elsewhere is any indication, many of the rural-suburban schools will employ a mix of programs to meet the needs of their students.

The Stand-Alone High-Scoring

These schools accept students only by test scores or teacher recommendations. They don't draw from the immediate neighborhood; they draw from throughout a school district or several school districts.

Not surprisingly, they include some of highest scoring schools in the state: Lowell in San Francisco, Whitney and the California Academy of Arts and Sciences in Los Angeles County, Troy in Fullerton (Orange County) and Pacific Collegiate in Santa Cruz.

More of these schools are coming, some as charters, which illustrates one of the enduring laws of education and life. What starts out one way — charters were introduced mainly to help low-scoring kids — may end up another, to serve the high achieving. Also known as the law of unintended consequences.

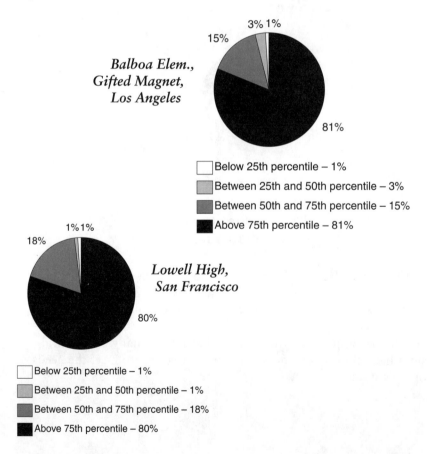

Balboa Elem.,
Gifted Magnet,
Los Angeles

3% 1%
15%
81%

☐ Below 25th percentile – 1%
▨ Between 25th and 50th percentile – 3%
▨ Between 50th and 75th percentile – 15%
■ Above 75th percentile – 81%

Lowell High,
San Francisco

1% 1%
18%
80%

☐ Below 25th percentile – 1%
▨ Between 25th and 50th percentile – 1%
▨ Between 50th and 75th percentile – 18%
■ Above 75th percentile – 80%

Whitney High, Los Angeles

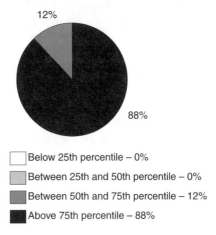

12%

88%

☐ Below 25th percentile – 0%

▦ Between 25th and 50th percentile – 0%

▨ Between 50th and 75th percentile – 12%

■ Above 75th percentile – 88%

High Scores Move Inland

Tracy in San Joaquin County is attracting many high-tech workers from Silicon Valley and Alameda County. Scores bounce all over but some schools are reaching the 70th and 80th percentiles.

Greater Sacramento provides even more striking examples. In the 1980s, the region, because of its low land prices, attracted many high-tech firms and technical employees, often well educated.

Schools in places like Roseville, Granite Bay, Rocklin, Folsom and El Dorado Hills are hitting the 80th and 90th percentiles.

In Southern California, cities such as Santa Clarita, Temecula, Murrieta, Corona and the Chino area have seen their scores rocket in the last 20 years.

Many schools in these areas are in transition. They change as their demographics change.

The Arguments

When you read the preceding it might seem compellingly logical that every school would structure its programs according to the abilities of its students. It just doesn't work that way.

Many schools and teachers are uneasy about or flat opposed to breaking kids out by ability — a practice called tracking — because this often means you divide by ethnicity or race. Many parents of those in the slower group think this is racism or unfair.

The disaffected also includes parents whose kids score about the middle. They might reason that their kids are being sacrificed to the slower pace while others are exempted.

It is almost Biblical truth among parents and educators that the children will do better if they could only be "challenged," or placed in a more demanding setting. And there is enough substance to this to justify the belief.

Breaking out or clustering sometimes costs extra money. Take a school with many kids scoring low and a few scoring high. The top group may not produce enough students to fill a class or a program; the advanced classes might have to be subsidized.

Schools are under increasing pressure to do a better job of educating the poor, the disadvantaged and low-scoring minorities, and to mainstream them — to educate them within the regular classroom.

This is one of the strengths of the middle or middle-plus schools. Their children score across the spectrum so often it is possible to blend kids of varying abilities within one classroom. The teacher can aim the instruction at the middle yet find the time to work with the slower and faster kids. Where the middle is thin, where there is a wide divergence between high and low scoring, the teacher's job becomes difficult.

Tracking And Differentiated Instruction

Despite misgivings, some school districts resort to tracking and many teachers, no matter what the school, use a technique called "differentiated instruction."

The teacher breaks out the class informally. Readers at one table, slow readers at another, non-readers at a third.

Each group can advance at its own pace and the teacher can address the needs of each group. If the advanced finishes its assignment, it can be given other work.

Sometimes a child will be strong in one subject and weak in another. The poor reader excels at math. For part of the day, he would be with the slow readers, for part, the advanced math. For general activities, for play, the class comes together as one.

At the third grade, many schools identify "gifted" students. These students are pulled out of class every week for a few hours of advanced instruction and within the class, they might be clustered to work at a fast pace.

Differentiated instruction gives the teacher flexibility to deal with students with varying needs. But even that might be difficult pull off. If most of the kids need remedial or a lot of attention, the teacher might find it difficult to break out groups. She might aim all instruction at the approximate middle of the class. Some schools enlist the faster students to help with the slower. But this risks parental anger.

Accidental Tracking

Often tracking doesn't start as tracking — clustering by ability.

It sometimes begins as grouping the children by programs or interests. A magnet program that stresses science and has a demanding curriculum might attract mainly high-achieving students.

A school might start a program for limited-English students and find that the classes attract many low-achieving students — who may be low achieving in part because they have trouble with English.

A few programs pop up almost out of the blue. They have some hidden qualifier that clusters the high achieving for at least part of the day. Programs like this show up in districts where the school is balancing extremes: high scoring and low scoring and a thin middle.

High schools almost have to practice tracking. To meet the needs of the university-bound students, the schools have to offer demanding college-prep classes. These classes may be limited to students who have a certain grade-point average. Even if the classes are open to all students, many middle- and low-achieving students may avoid them for fear they would not be able to do the work.

For overt tracking, sometimes the school district finds it hard to resist parental pressures and the logic of allowing students to learn as fast they can.

The Parents

Let's assume that you are an active parent and your daughter scores in the 80th percentile, top 20 percent. You chat with co-workers or relatives and find out that their second-graders have learned how to multiply and are working on division.

You say, what's going on here? My kid is still working on multiplication.

You talk to the teacher and look at the class scores, readily available, and find out that the class is still on multiplication because the kids are slow learners and many of them are landing below the 25th percentile.

You say to the teacher, "I want my daughter to learn as fast as she is able."

The teacher replies, "I'll do my best but because most of the class is struggling with multiplication, I must concentrate on their needs."

A reasonable answer. No villains here.

But to you an unacceptable answer. You talk to other parents with high-achieving kids and find out that they too are unhappy.

You band together and go to the principal and say, We want changes. You also complain to the school board and the superintendent.

The School's Reaction

The principal might say, "I'm sorry; I see the problem but we want to blend the kids across achievement levels and besides we don't have the money to break out smaller classes. I'll speak to the teacher; maybe she can organize the class to move some students at a faster pace."

You and your group reply, "We're going to place our kids in private schools."

Maybe you're bluffing but the principal takes a second look at your group and sees his most active parents, the people who volunteer for projects, who show up for school events, who make sure their kids do their homework. He knows that if the school loses this group it will suffer. He also knows that the overall scores will drop and when scores drop the school's reputation drops.

Meanwhile, school trustees talk to the superintendent and she calls the principal and says in so many words, "I'm getting some heat. Let's get together and kick around a few ideas."

And one day, lo and behold, a class or classes appear that include almost all the advanced kids. Or the school creates a school within a school.

Or to take a recent change in Northern California, the school district dropped a magnet program that blended kids and went to neighborhood schools, an arrangement that usually leads to ability grouping. The district also introduced advanced classes into the high school.

These are not win-win scenarios. In this case, a principal and two vice-principals resigned, warning that the new policies will cause segregation by ethnicity.

The Los Angeles District, which is trying to meet the needs of a quite diverse student body, has created gifted schools and a variety of magnet schools.

Selfish Parents?

They don't see it that way. They see themselves as champions of their children. They see themselves as parents who work hard at education and they don't think their kids should be penalized because they show up prepared and other kids don't.

Many of these parents will understand that the affluent schools don't have to deal with these problems, that they can concentrate on pushing their kids ahead.

When it comes to college admissions, these parents know that their children will be judged on their grades and scores and not on whether they slowed down to help classmates.

Parental ambition comes in a variety of forms.

One Southern California district with many minorities and low-scoring students has created fundamental schools that require parent participation. These schools teach their students, many of them from low-income homes, in regular classes but because they require parents to take the initiative in applying, they may be screening out the less energetic parents, and this will influence scores.

So popular are these schools that for years, until the application process was revised, parents camped out at nights to get their children admitted.

Passions

Often they run high. In 2003, a group of parents stormed the office of superintendent of San Francisco schools, protesting a policy that sent their kids out of the neighborhood schools.

Many parents don't protest; they just move to a different district. Or they shop for homes in districts with at least middling plus scores. Or they transfer or lie their way — phony address or guardian — into another district.

In Berkeley many parents send the young children to private schools for the elementary and middle grades, then to the public high school where a lot of program conflicts play out. Berkeley High is notoriously stressful and has gone through several principals in a few years.

San Francisco has the highest percentage of private school students of any county in the state.

Berkeley and San Francisco are politically liberal and down through the years have approved many bond issues for the public schools. But although they support the idea of public schools, even liberal parents are leery about placing their own children in low-scoring or troubled schools.

Single-Sex Classes

There are not many but they are there. The theory, ancient in origin, is that the boys will learn more if they are not distracted by girls, and vice versa.

Over the last 25 years, girls have done much better in school than boys (but not in all subjects). At many universities, women outnumber men by ratios that often approach three women for every two men

Some researchers are starting to ask, "What's with boys?" The future might bring more single-sex classes.

What's A Parent To Do?

If you have waded this far, you may be pulling your hair out. California schools seem so complex.

Many are but this stuff has going on probably since Socrates held class in the marketplace. Name the state or country and you will find parents maneuvering to get their kids into certain schools or fiddling with programs and curriculum to advance the interests of their children.

These days, thanks to computers, the game is much more out in the open. California schools, in their SARC reports and other literature, do a good job of presenting their scores and describing their programs.

What the schools don't do is dwell on the problems of pacing and academic intensity. To be fair to the schools, it's hard for them to deal with these issues.

The simple and unpleasant truth is that many children come to school unprepared or poorly prepared and get little or no academic support from their parents and friends.

Lest this sound totally discouraging, scores seem to be rising. More students are coming up to what the state deems proficient. But many schools still score low or below proficiency. The state, assessing results in 2004, placed 74 percent of the elementary schools below the proficiency grade of 800. The "below" figure for the middle schools was 84 percent and for the high schools 93 percent. (Keep in mind that many students at the "below" schools are scoring above 800).

Schools have to pace themselves, have to structure their programs, to some degree, to the level of their students.

You can argue that the parents and the peers are not to blame, that in many instances they have been treated shabbily, even horribly, by life and history. As individuals and as a society we should work to correct injustices and make our schools better and more effective.

But education, in many instances, is a here and now business. If your child is attending school, the quality of his or her education depends on what happens now, not what reforms bring years in the future.

What the school or school setting lacks, you may have to provide. What's good for your kids will almost always be good for the school. Some suggestions:

Advice

• *Kindergarten ready.* If the kids start out behind, they may stay behind. If you can't do it by yourself (or even if you can), enroll the child in a good preschool. The same for reading to the children and other activities that nourish the brain. As parents, the authors can testify that kids like the dumbest stuff read to them over and over. Absolute torture! Do what you can and if you can't do much, take them to the library and look for other ways to move them along.

• *Make friends with the teacher.* Yes some are pills but many become teachers because they like kids and want to improve their lives. If your child is having trouble, the teacher might move him to a different part of the class or simply give him extra attention. Or give you good advice.

• *Ask for the good teachers.* You might not always get the best but if the school knows you're savvy about teachers, it might not stick your kid with the worst. See Chapter 3.

• *Watch the pacing.* The standards spell out in detail what the kids should be learning. Check them.

• *Show up for Back-to-School Nights and Open House.* Studies suggest that if you take education and school seriously, it will rub off on the kids. Some of the events you'll enjoy: the school play, the band recital, the sports.

• *Read the school literature.* Check out the Web site. There might be a homework club. Or some service that offers academic help over the Web.

• *Make sure the homework gets done.*

• *Gossip and chit chat.* Talk to your friends and co-workers. Find out what's going on in their schools. If you can tap into your school's gossip, do so. Join the PTA. Work in the snack shack and get to know parents. Gossip can be faulty but often it's how you identify good teachers.

• *Buy Help.* When you're weary, it's hard to do the school stuff. Some parents are temperamentally unsuited to helping their kids. Ask the teacher about tutoring. She may know of some parent who wants to pick up a few bucks. Or even a responsible high school or college student. See the phone directory, under Tutoring.

• *Vote for all school-tax increases.* Really! Compared to other states, our funding is behind. Education is not like building widgets. You can't speed up the line. You can't use robots. You have to put a living, breathing teacher in the classroom. It's expensive.

• *More money, money.* Many schools will have parent clubs or education foundations. You donate to them and they spread the money where they think it will do the most good. Or you work in the snack shack and give the proceeds to the school.
One of these years when you're old and gray and the kids have finished college or landed good jobs, you'll be able to stand tall and say:
"Welcome to Wal-Mart."
"Would you like fries with that burger?"
(Stop whimpering! It's for the children.)

• *Ask for advice.* If your child is falling behind, ask for a conference with a teacher or administrator. If you can't meet the teacher, call or e-mail. Some contact is better than none.

• *Look for Free Enrichment Activities.* Many community colleges run summer fun academic classes for the kids. Some city recreation departments offer many activities, especially in summer, for toddlers, adolescents and teens.

• *If the classroom or the teacher is not working,* ask for a change. Some things are not meant to be. Move on.

• *The same for the school.* It just might be a bad fit. If it can't deliver what your child needs, ask for a transfer. Or move. Or if you have the money, try a private school.

7

Alternative Education

- ACADEMIES
- CONTINUATION HIGH
- MIDDLE COLLEGE HIGH
- GIFTED PROGRAMS

- CHARTER SCHOOLS
- MAGNET SCHOOLS
- ARTS SCHOOLS
- UNUSUAL PROGRAMS

Overview

This chapter lists and explains many of the programs and alternatives to regular school. Some of these programs address the needs of children who are having problems and for this reason this chapter overlaps somewhat with Chapter 9 on special education. See also Vocational Education, Chapter 8.

California school districts long ago realized that some students did not fit in the regular program and so they created special programs. In recent decades, the number of separate approaches has multiplied, sometimes for political reasons, other times social and academic.

Many of these programs and schools have no relation to one another.

As a rule, the larger the district, the more numerous the programs.

Magnet Schools

Many of these schools got their start in the 1970s and 1980s as a way to integrate districts without forced busing.

Segregation usually follows housing patterns. One ethnic group lives in one neighborhood, another in a second neighborhood, a third in another neighborhood and so on. Almost all school districts assign children to their neighborhood schools and this segregates the schools by the ethnicity of the neighborhood.

To woo parents and students away from their neighborhood schools and mix the kids, the districts enriched the programs of certain schools. The offerings included high-tech and computer programs, international studies, science, foreign languages and performing arts. All the schools retained their core programs; the goodies were added. The district told parents, we know you want to stay with the local school but if you transfer here or there, your child will get a better education. Often free busing was provided.

Many magnet schools are still employed for this purpose: to mix the students by race. But as time passed, some of these schools married other goals or interests and became something else. Among the most popular, which we will mention separately, the performing arts school.

Also academies or schools within a school. See academies.

Charter schools, introduced in the 1990s, embraced, if unintentionally, part of the magnet concept. See charters in this chapter.

Academies

Also called learning communities or houses. After promoting large high schools for years, the educational community in the 1990s soured on some aspects of these schools. They thought that many students got "lost" in the maze of classes and programs.

To counteract this, some large high schools divided their operations into academies. In a typical arrangement, the school identifies popular programs — technology, food service, multimedia — and assigns students and teachers to each program. The teachers and the students come to know each other better, the focus is sharper.

When students have to take general education classes that require reading this book or writing that paper, the assignments can be tied into the programs, for example, a computer student might write a paper about computers.

Performing Arts Academies

Many large high schools these days have their own performing arts academies, a cluster of classes within the school that concentrates on the arts.

Some large districts have gone a step beyond: whole schools devoted to the arts or the performing arts.

Among the most popular: the Orange County High School of

the Arts, the San Diego School of Creative and Performing Arts, and in San Francisco, the School of the Arts.

At least some of these schools welcome students from outside their districts (but you have to provide the transportation).

If your child is interested in this kind of school ask your school counselor what's available. In some cases, students must audition or in some other way demonstrate the sincerity of their interest.

Some of these schools are charters. Some may be functioning as magnet schools.

High-Tech High Schools

There are several of these around the state including Napa's New Technology High and San Diego's High-Tech High. One is an alternative school and the other a charter.

The schools offer curriculums focusing on science, math and engineering with the intent of preparing students for careers in high tech. These schools were opened at the prompting of businesses. They complained that the regular schools were not preparing students for jobs in high tech.

Middle College High School

The school district identifies students who can do the work but are not; they're underperforming. It then works with the local community college to create a high-school program on the college campus.

The hope is that the college setting will inspire the kids to shape up and start thinking about college. This approach also brings in the advantages of the academy: The students are assigned their own teachers, the program focus sharpens. Another plus: The students are removed from their old campuses, where, for whatever reason, they did not thrive academically.

Fundamental Schools

Some of these schools were started in the 1970s when parents, disappointed in the educational experiments of that era, pressured the local school boards to create structured schools that concentrated on the basics. "Structure" is a relative term. A few schools tightened up in discipline, adopted a dress code and paid more attention to the basics but kept the regular program.

Other fundamentals notched up the structure and exacted promises from parents that they would play an active role in their child's education.

Among the more popular models: the fundamentals of the Santa Ana Unified School District in Orange County. Until the enrollment procedure was changed, parents camped out to get their kids into these schools and even now there's a rush to gain admission.

Charter Schools

The charter idea got its start in the school battles of the late 20th century. Many people and educators lost confidence in the public schools, especially those that year in and out scored low. The thinking took hold that the schools themselves were at fault, that they had become crippled with senseless rules and regulations, that somehow the unions were to blame, and that the solution lay in freeing the schools from many of these restraints.

One part of the movement favored vouchers: giving parents a tuition voucher and allowing them to transfer to any school of their choice, including private or religious schools (usually non-union). In some states, the voucher battles still are being fought; California voted against vouchers.

The other part went for charters, which allowed parents and districts to start or designate schools that would be free of many restrictions but in some aspects remain public.

In the early 1990s, the California Legislature passed a bill creating a limited number of charters. Since then over 460 schools have opened as charters or switched from regular public to charter public.

The unions warily accepted charters except those that undermined or somehow threatened the union contract. At least two did, one in Sacramento, the other in San Francisco. In Sacramento, the union sued the school, which nonetheless opened after a compromise was reached barring new charters without teachers being consulted. In San Francisco, after a long battle, a similar compromise was worked out and the school operator agreed not to open another school in the district.

The unions won legislation that forbade existing private schools from converting to charters; charter status would allow them to draw state funds. Religious schools cannot be designated charter schools. Charters can be closed if they fail to meet state accountability standards.

Charters were presented as rescue schools for the low-achieving and to a large extent they have remained true to this mission.

But middle- and high-achieving schools also have gone the charter route. At a few school districts, when parents wanted a Montessori, they convinced administrators to turn regular schools into Montessori charters.

At one high school in Southern California, parents became disenchanted with the school administration. So, to get control of matters, they switched their school to a charter. Very little was changed in the school's programs.

In Oakland, Mayor Jerry Brown implored the local school district to create a military charter and give the kids a regimen of discipline. Oakland is very liberal: it did not like the idea of a military school. Brown went around the local school board and secured a charter from Sacramento. Oakland now has a military charter school that answers to an agency in the Dept. of Education.

A few charter schools have closed and more probably will. Having a decade of experience with charters, the politicians are getting a better idea of what's acceptable.

Nonetheless, the charter idea is very much alive and takes in some of the most interesting schools in the state. They include:

Aspire Schools

Ten schools located in or near low-income neighborhoods in Oakland, East Palo Alto, Stockton-Lodi and Modesto. Aspire presents itself as an entrepreneurial-innovative venture that solves problems and gets results. This sounds trite but it reflects a business orientation — if it doesn't work we're going to drop it and find something that does. Keep in mind the rap against public schools is that they hold onto methods that don't seem to work.

Aspire is also into standards and assessments and structure and more time in school (more and longer days). And it has bought into another movement: small schools. For kindergarten-through-5th-grade schools, no more than 360 students, for grades 6 to 12, no more than 420.

Aspire is backed by Bill Gates of Microsoft. For information, www.aspirepublicschools.org. or (650) 637-2062.

Edison Schools

Edison runs or helps manage at least eight elementary or middle schools in California: in Chula Vista, East Palo Alto (2), Fresno, Long Beach, Napa, San Francisco and West Covina. Some of these schools are run in partnerships with the local school district.

In San Francisco, Edison got into a hellacious argument with the school board and the unions that was resolved by securing a charter from the state and coming out from under the control of the San Francisco Unified School District. Edison promised not to open another school in San Francisco.

Edison is run for profit and at least some of its schools offer a pay package that differs from the unions package. For this and other reasons, unions perceive it as a threat.

Edison schools do not charge tuition. As public schools, they get their money from state funds. Edison teaching days and teaching years run longer than most public schools. Like all public schools these days, Edison's must meet the state's assessment standards but Edison agrees with and practices assessment methods.

Edison was one of the first "private" systems to take on public schools and over the years it has changed its methods. Each school manages its own calendar.

For information on Edison schools, go to www.edisonschools.com.

KIPP Schools

KIPP stands for Knowledge Is Power Program. It was started by two Texas teachers who thought that public-school methods were not working.

KIPP bases its program on what it calls the Five Pillars. They are:

- **High expectations.** Informal rewards and punishments. No excuses mentality. Silence. No candy. Uniforms. Structure.

- **Choice and commitment.** Parents and kids must sign onto the program. Math and reading, music and art.

- **More time.** Classes from 7 a.m. to 5 p.m. Saturday school. Summer school.

- **Principals with power.** They control their budgets and make assignments as they see fit. Principals train for one year at UC Berkeley Haas School of Business.
- **Focus on results.** Standardized tests. Objective measures. Goal is to get students into college. Most of students come from low-income neighborhoods.

Among backers: State and feds; these are public schools. Don Fisher, founder of the Gap clothing.

Schools are located in Los Angeles (2), San Diego, San Francisco (2), San Lorenzo, Oakland and Sacramento. More are planned.

Note tie to Haas School of Business. This is another instance of schools turning away from educational management models and embracing business models.

For information, www.kipp.org.

University Sponsored or Helped

UC San Diego sponsors the Preuss School, a middle school-high school located on the UC campus. Preuss is part of UC effort to prepare low-income, often minority students for college. (See following, UC Outreach). The school was built with private money; the land was provided by the university. The school, a charter, is funded mainly through the San Diego Unified School District. The university provides student tutors and help in a variety of forms, access to libraries and computers, assistance with curriculum planning and counseling, encouragement of the arts.

Some universities have partnerships or arrangements, often informal, with local public schools but do not involve themselves deeply in the management of the schools.

The University of Southern California (USC) has sort of adopted a K-12 school in its neighborhood. The lower grades run a performing arts program, the upper, a math-science-technology program. USC, which also helps other schools, lets this K-12 use its classrooms and sports facilities and funds an afterschool program in the arts. The university also pays for projects that put volunteers in the school. The USC School of Social Work assigns two interns to counsel the school's kids and parents.

Other universities, especially those with teaching programs, help similarly with the local schools.

University of California Outreach

In 1996, through Proposition 209, California voters shot down the University of California's program of admitting students according to their race. The university stepped up a program of encouraging and educating low-income students, many of them from ethnic groups underrepresented at the UCs. In this way, the UC hoped to raise the number of the underrepresented without getting trapped in the snares of racial choosing.

The UC system established partnerships with elementary and high schools located in low-income areas around the state, offered them advice on the UC programs, funded scholarships and academic programs and encouraged the students to apply to a UC.

Although aimed at the disadvantaged, these programs at the selected schools are open to all.

For more information, www.ucop.edu and hit K-12 educators.

Tough-Admission Academic Schools

Several high schools around the state and some elementary schools admit students according to grades and how well they do on a test. These schools score among the tops in the state and in the nation.

At least one of these schools — Lowell in San Francisco — has been doing this for close to 100 years.

Others have embraced the practice because parents argued that their children should be allowed to learn as fast as they can. In some situations, these students attended low-scoring schools that put their efforts into remedial work. The parents of the high achieving said it was not fair to pace the fast learners to the remedial.

The schools include some gifted magnets in the Los Angeles Unified School District, which runs a variety of programs.

It also includes Whitney High in Cerritos and the California Academy of Math and Science in Carson (Los Angeles County); Troy High and the Oxford Academy in Cypress (Orange County); Pacific Collegiate Charter in Santa Cruz.

Gifted And Talented Students

Most of California's school districts operate programs for intellectually gifted or creatively talented students, known as GATE (Gifted and Talented Education). These are high-scoring students often bored with the regular curriculum and able to handle more demanding work.

GATE provides these challenges in specific academic areas, leadership, visual and performing arts and creativity. The state gives grants to schools to create advanced placement and honors programs.

In some schools, where the number of gifted students doesn't justify the expense of creating a GATE program, eligible students can take classes at the local community college or specialized classes online.

GATE Eligibility

To qualify as gifted and talented, a student must demonstrate leadership in specific academics or the arts. IQ alone won't hack it. The state recommends against IQ tests, contending they measure only a narrow range of creative or academic ability and can be racially biased.

Instead, the state recommends several measures, including achievement, standardized test scores, motivation, recommendations from parents and teachers and peers, classroom observation and portfolio assessment.

Community Day Schools

Operated by districts and county offices of education to help students who have been expelled from school. Staff usually includes counselors and mental health therapists as well as teachers, all of whom are trained in pupil discipline. Students attend school for a minimum of six hours and focus on academics, self-esteem and social skills.

County Community Schools

This is for kids in trouble and under the supervision of probation officers, juvenile court or the local school district. These students have been expelled by their local districts or might be homeless or have been referred by the courts or probation departments. The schools are run by the county office of education. Students attend class four hours a day and work on academics, social skills, self-discipline and getting along with others.

Continuation High Schools

These schools are for high-school students 16 to 18 years old who are in danger of dropping or failing out of school. Usually these students have failed previous courses and are behind their peers on the number of credits needed to graduate. Offering a mix of academic courses that combine classes on life skills with work experience, these schools provide a stable, relaxed environment allowing students to complete their courses satisfactorily. Students are in class for three hours each day.

Independent Study

Students study at home, completing assignments developed with their teacher and in accordance with the curriculum. They meet periodically with the teacher to review their work and get new assignments. The teacher is available by telephone during the rest of the time. Many students schedule their independent study around their work. Child actors, Olympic athletes, the chronically-ill and students who for a variety of reasons cannot stand regular school are some of those enrolled. The state department of education has published the "Independent Study Operations Manual" detailing how the program works. Call (800) 995-4099.

Language Schools Or Programs

Many schools with students who speak little or no English offer a variety of language transition or improvement programs. See discussion in Chapter 4, Curriculum.

Community Colleges

Many high school students take classes at the local community college. These classes often meet the admission requirements of the universities.

In the summer, community colleges often run low-cost classes and activities for the children— a good way to give them an academic boost.

Vocational Programs and Job Training

See Chapter 8.

Adult Schools

Almost all the school districts run adult schools that enroll hundreds and often thousands. Many classes are aimed at working people who want to learn new skills so they can advance at the job or secure a new job. Or improve their fluency in English. For information, contact your local school district. See Chapter 8.

Small Schools

Educational researchers argue that small schools do a better job than big schools. Some school districts, with private funds, plan to open a number of these schools in the next few years. Enrollments would top out at 500.

Cyber School

California has at least one, the California Virtual Academy.

The kids are educated by computer and get their lessons and classes over the Internet from a program put together by William Bennett, who served the Reagan White House as Secretary of Education. Bennett has been a steady critic of public schools and their unions. Guess what? Cyber School is running into opposition. But being new and untested, the Virtual Academy was going to be greeted with much skepticism.

The Virtual Academy and its offspring came as state charters, meaning they were eligible for state funds. But several have lost their charter status.

A surprising number of California parents educate their children at home. For those interested in the approach, the Virtual Academy might be helpful.

For more information, go to www.caliva.org.

8

Vocational Education

- ADULT EDUCATION
- WHEN KIDS CAN WORK
- AGRICULTURE
- COMMUNITY COLLEGES

It used to be a kid could drop out of school and join the military. No longer, however. Uncle Sam still wants you— but only if you have the right skills.

Our society is so dependent upon skilled labor that few of the unskilled can get work beyond flipping burgers. Most gas stations are self-service and many pumps are designed to take cash or plastic, eliminating even the cashier. Yet someone has to know how to fix the pumps when they crash.

Many school districts have a vocational program for students whose goal is to get a job. Some programs allow students to focus on academics and work, others offer hands-on training in everything from animal husbandry to network cable technology.

The technicians who install and service your cable network, the stylist who cuts your hair, the mechanic who repairs your car, the chef who cooks your dinner, the waiter who serves it, the draftsman who prepares the blueprints for your house — they represent just some of the trades being taught in high schools.

Some programs are offered through adult education, others in conjunction with the Regional Occupational Programs (often called R-O-P) or through partnerships with local community colleges. Even students living in rural areas have many training choices and not just in agriculture.

Many schools offer job-interviewing classes, job-shadowing where students select a business person to observe for a day and in-school visits by various professionals to discuss their careers.

When Students Can Work

Any student between the ages of 13 and 18, with parents' permission, may obtain a work permit from the local school district. All applicants must have a Social Security card. The student's job must not interfere with attendance or performance at school or the permit will be revoked. Work time is restricted:

- **13-year-olds:** two hours daily up to four per week. The student must have finished the sixth grade, be identified as a potential dropout and participating in a district-sponsored work program at school; eight hours per day up to 40 per week during summer vacation

- **14- to 15-year-olds:** three hours daily up to 18 per week or 23 per week if the student is enrolled in a work-experience program; eight hours per day up to 40 per week during summer vacation.

- **16- to 17-year-olds:** no more than four hours daily or eight hours on a non-school day; eight hours per day up to 48 per week during summer vacation.

Minimum wage for teens is $6.75 an hour.

Some jobs are off-limits, including those where alcohol or tobacco products are served or sold.

ROP Classes

If college is not your kid's ambition, then investigate enrolling him in an ROP.

Regional Occupational Programs teach job skills to high-school students aged 16 and older, along with adult students. Usually, the student attends regular class in the morning and trade classes in the afternoon. Training takes place in the classroom or at business sites.

Among the trades: cosmetology, metalworking, network cable technology, eldercare, office work, medical positions and computers.

In addition, students get placement assistance, job counseling and other services to make them self-supporting when they leave high school. Talk to your school officials to obtain more information. You may have to rent or buy some tools.

Agriculture And ROP

Over 300 high schools and colleges offer agricultural programs ranging from agriculture biology to tractor restoration. Typical offerings might include:

- Agriculture Business and Marketing
- Agricultural Biotechnician and Technology
- Agricultural Computers
- Agricultural Equipment Maintenance and Operation
- Advanced Livestock Management
- Agricultural Sales & Services
- Agricultural Technology
- Agricultural Welding and Construction
- Agricultural Zoology
- Animal and Veterinary Careers
- Dairy Management
- Farm Power Mechanics
- Floriculture
- Forestry Resource Management
- Green House Management
- Landscape Maintenance and Nursery Technology
- Livestock and Meat Processing

Other Choices

The following are typical of many of the courses ROP offers throughout the state:

- Advanced Business Computer Applications
- Accounting Clerk
- Advanced Welding
- Applied Auto Engineering
- Auto Body and Fender Repair
- Building Trades
- Computer Maintenance Technician
- Desktop Publishing
- Electronic Technician

- Entrepreneurship/Small Business Operation
- Fire-Fighting Technology
- Nurses Assistant
- Photography
- Police Science
- Retail Sales/Merchandising
- Word Processing

Community Colleges And Vocational Training

Community colleges offer a wide array of courses and certificate programs covering jobs skills for the first-time workers or for adults who want upgrade skills or add new ones. These classes include:

- Accounting
- Appliance Repair
- Business
- Carpentry
- Computer Operations and Repairs
- Construction
- Counseling
- Corrections (Jails and Prisons) and Police Academy
- Culinary Arts and Restaurant Management
- Dental Assisting
- Early Childhood Education
- Fiber Optics
- Foster Care Education
- Nursing and Emergency Care
- Nutrition
- Office: Clerical and Secretarial
- Plumbing
- Welding Technology

ROP Or Adult Education

There is almost no difference between many of the classes in ROP or adult education. In fact, one probably could find the same person teaching in ROP and adult education. ROP classes are for both high-school students and adults while adult education serves only people 18 or older.

Adult classes range from firefighting and public safety to computer technology and medical office work, English as a second language, basic education and GED classes. See Chapter 5 for information on the GED.

Many people in adult ed classes are pursuing a GED or a high-school diploma by taking the same classes they would have taken in high school. Often, however, these adults have done poorly in math or reading or English. They take classes to bolster these skills so they can take the advanced courses needed to get their diplomas. These programs are funded by the state and federal government.

Additionally, adult ed offers classes for people who have a high school diploma. These classes might cover aspects of firefighting, police work and office operations. Some of these classes charge fees.

Adult ed also covers personal enrichment, such as line dancing, yoga, exercise and the arts, and classes on improving one's life: parenting, getting organized, etc. Many of the enrichment classes are aimed at the elderly.

Adult Education Costs

Many adult ed classes are free. For fee classes, here's a sampling of what you might pay:

- Clinical medical assistant, $895 (includes books, medical equipment and internship).
- Phlebotomy, $295 (includes books, medical equipment and internship)
- Introduction to Personal Computer, $60
- Basic watercolor, $25
- The stock market, $20
- Beginning folk guitar, $50
- Knitting workshop, $40

Private Vocational Training

Many private firms, notably Heald and DeVrys, offer vocational training and job placement.

The University of California and the California State University, through their extension programs, offer some classes that fall into the category of vocational.

Check your phone directory under Schools.

Military Programs

The military has a program known as "College First," allowing students who qualify to enlist, graduate and defer the military commitment for up to two years while they attend college. For more information about this and other military assistance programs see www.cde.ca.gov/ci/military.html.

Military Recruiters

State law requires any school that allows job recruiters to come on campus also must allow military recruiters. Students who are not interested in military service, however, can choose not to meet with them.

Home Economics

Thing of the past. Very few schools offer what once was popular in California schools. We know of one school that invested in a modern and well-equipped kitchen and a few years later tore it out. At least some teachers would like to bring back Home Ec. Another complaint voiced by several teachers we talked to: vocational ed is being sacrificed to academics. They say that many students will go into the trades and will not need such subjects as algebra.

9

Special Education

When a child's mental or physical condition interferes with his ability to learn, he may be placed in a program that falls under the category of special education.

Many of these programs keep the child in the regular class and pull him out for a few hours a week for instruction designed to correct or ameliorate his condition. Nonetheless, for mild or serious disabilities, about the same evaluation procedure is followed.

Screening and Evaluation

• The teacher, especially in the early grades, detects a condition that might qualify the child for special education. She requests an evaluation. Parents, even before the child starts school, can ask for an evaluation. The school reviews these requests and makes a decision whether to evaluate. If it denies the request, parents can appeal.

• Before an evaluation is made, parents must give permission.

• The evaluation is done within the framework of federal legislation, notably the Individuals with Disabilities Education Act. The law defines the categories of disability:

- Autism
- Deafness
- Other hearing impairments
- Cognitive delay
- Multiple disabilities
- Orthopedic impairment
- Other health impairments
- Traumatic brain injury
- Other visual impairments

• The evaluation is done. It might include looking at your child's health, vision, hearing, social and emotional well-being, general intelligence, school performance, his body movements and how well he communicates with others.

The evaluation is done by a team that can include the teacher, a child psychologist, a special education person, the parents, a school representative who knows what services the school or district can offer, a testing person who can explain the evaluation and make recommendations and possibly a representative of a social agency.

• The evaluation team decides whether the child qualifies for special education. If special education is rejected, the team might recommend different classroom tactics or, say, reading help.

• Individualized Education Program. If the team agrees that the child can benefit from special education, it draws up an Individualized Education Program to help the child deal with the specific disability or disabilities and secure a good education.

• Follow up. Special education students must be reevaluated at least every three years. This evaluation reviews the progress of the child and decides whether he should continue in the program.

Serious Disabilities

Parents with preschool children who obviously are developmentally disabled and are not already in a program through a regional center for the disabled should contact the regional center in their area or the local school district. For the name and number of the regional center near you, call the California Department of Developmental Services at (916) 654-1690 or the Association of Regional Center Agencies at (916) 446-7961 or go to www.arcanet.org.

The Controversies

Special education may be no more contentious than any other field of education but at times it appears to upset an inordinate number of parents and educators. Some of the discontent comes from the infancy of special education. Many of the programs are new or fairly new and will need to be refined as experience indicates. Researchers and educators are still learning much about disabilities.

We are going to list and briefly explain some of the arguments. But much will be made clear by the following numbers from a 2004 edition of Education Week/Pew Foundation:

• About 9 percent of California children age 6 to 17 years are enrolled in a special education program. When ages 3 to 5 and 18 to 21 are included, the percentage rises to 10.5 percent of all between ages 3 and 21.

• Special education funding varies widely by state and up-to-date information is lagging but from 1999 data it appears that California, above regular costs, spends an average $7,500 annually per special education student. About 60 percent of the special ed money comes from the state and feds; about 40 percent from local sources (source Education Week).

• Special Education students in California, according to their disabilities, divide as follows (rounded):
   - Specific learning disabilities, 56 percent. Of this group expanded nationally, about 80 percent of the problems concern inability to read.
   - Speech or language impediments, 22 percent
   - Mental retardation, 6 percent
   - Emotional disturbance, 4 percent
   - Multiple disabilities, 1 percent
   - Hearing, 2 percent
   - Orthopedic, 2 percent
   - Other health impairments, 4 percent
   - Visual, 1 percent
   - Autism, 3 percent.

• **Money.** About 1990, when the federal government passed legislation ordering states to provide special education, critics were quick to point out that the feds were not adequately funding the law. In the 1990s, California struggled to fund adequately regular programs and special education. The special ed parents sued the state (and some school districts) and reached an uneasy compromise, which may unravel because of the state funding crisis.

• **The evolution of research.** Researchers say they are getting better at identifying and treating disabilities but their new techniques for some subgroups are more expensive.

- **Evaluations.** Worried about costs, at least some schools and districts are narrowly interpreting screening and evaluation guidelines. If you think your child suffers from some kind of attention deficit disorder, the local school might not evaluate for this malady. You might have to seek advice from your doctor or informally from the teacher (if she is willing to give an opinion).

- **Evaluation time.** Some evaluations take two or three days and tie up sometimes five people plus the parents.

- **Mainstreaming versus special classes.** A battle that probably never will be resolved. In California, according to the Education Week report, about 52 percent of the special-ed students spend about 80 percent of their time in regular class rooms and 26 percent of special-ed students are educated in their own groups for 60 percent of the school day.

- **Diagnosing Difficulties.** Loaded with data, researchers are able to break out the differences between ethnic groups and the sexes. Boys are more likely to be placed in special ed than girls and this raises the question whether boys are more prone to disabilities or by nature more likely to misbehave. For ethnic groups, one state took a second look at evaluation techniques and concluded that 9 percent of one ethnic group was in need of better regular instruction, not special ed.

- **Assessment.** Should special-ed students be given their own tests or the tests given to all students? It might seem obvious to give them their own tests but some educators argue that we should expect the same effort for one group as the other.

More Information?

In presenting the preceding, we have simplified the procedures to provide an overview of how screening and evaluation works. Most schools will give detailed packets on evaluations and special education. And what the schools lack, other organizations will provide. A good source: the National Information Center for Children and Youth with Disabilities, www.nichcy.org.

For the Education Week/Pew Foundation report, Jan.8, 2004, which gives a good overview of the many of the arguments, send $10 to Education Week. P.O. Box 2083, Marion OH 43306.

10

School Financing

- **BONDS AND TAXES**
- **SUPPLIES**
- **OTHER EXPENSES**
- **LOTTO MONEY**
- **PROM AND GRAD NITE**

Overview

When California had the money, it spent the money — on many programs, including education. In recent years, teacher salaries were elevated to the number one position among the 50 states and class sizes in the first four grades were lowered to no more than 20 students.

When California didn't have the money, when stocks and dot-coms crashed and government income dropped sharply, the state made minor cuts but essentially kept on spending. See chart at end of chapter.

This is the main reason why the state deficit soared to about $38 billion. To make up the deficit, programs will have to be cut and, no matter what Governor Schwarzenegger has promised, taxes will have to be raised.

Here's the word for the next few years — pain.

Just about every dog, cat, canary and human being in California knows that the way we tax and spend and fund the schools needs to be overhauled. Now that we have a crisis, some overdue changes may be made.

For parents, all this means that you will have to dig deeper or shoulder some of what the schools should be doing.

In fact, many parents, especially in affluent districts, long ago accepted the idea of a parent tax. These parents often want enriched programs and are willing to pay for them.

If you are not rolling in the bucks — and many parents are not — there are low-cost or free programs that can help your child. We will mention a few in this chapter.

K-12 Income and Expenses

Operational Revenues: $55.7 billion

- State funds, mostly sales and income taxes: $29.3 billion
- Local Property Taxes: $14.8 billion
- Local miscellaneous: developer fees, parcel-tax elections: $3.5 billion. The parcel taxes go to the districts that passed the tax. The developer fees usually to the district that imposed them.
- Federal government: $7.1 billion.
- Lottery, $800 million.

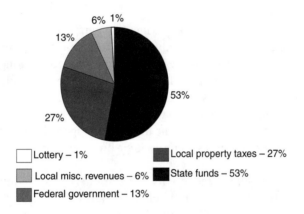

Lottery – 1% Local property taxes – 27%
Local misc. revenues – 6% State funds – 53%
Federal government – 13%

Construction Revenues

Capital improvements are generally funded by bonds. These are passed at the state level and by the local districts. At the state level, voters in 2002 approved bonds for $11.4 billion and in 2004 for $12.3 billion – money now working its way into the system.

Between 1998 and 2001, local districts, for their own needs passed 127 bond measures totaling $6.8 billion. At that time, they needed approval by two-thirds of the voters.

In 2001, a new law took effect, lowering the approval to 55 percent. This prompted many districts that had been turned down for a bond to try again. Between 2001 and 2004, the districts passed 159 bond measures, raising $12.3 billion.

Where The Money Is Spent

Precise figures are difficult because with the deficit crisis the state for many programs is budgeting one amount and allocating a smaller amount. The state has also borrowed money to deal with the deficit and deferred some payments. Some of these practices probably will continue until California figures out ways to handle the deficit.

To give the big picture, we are providing figures used in the 2003 budget.

• State funding of schools and districts, $29 billion. Each district receives a certain amount per student to pay for salaries and ordinary expenses. More on this later.

• State funding of categorical programs, $11 billion. This money goes for about 100 programs, from special education for the disabled through enriched instruction for the gifted to civics classes for immigrants.

• The federal funding, $7.1 billion, goes almost entirely to categorical projects chosen by the federal government. Almost all federal money goes to programs designed to help disadvantaged or special education students.

Why Sports Cost So Much

As parents of the student athlete, you will want to attend the home games and as many away games as possible. Beyond the costs of admission, there are incidental costs such as your gas and meals for attending away games. For outdoor games, bundle up and bring a cushion.

California Spending vs. Other States
Amount Spent Per Student, Public Schools

State	Total	State	Total
New York	$ 10,922	Georgia	$ 6,909
New Jersey	10,893	Montana	6,671
Washington D.C.	10,852	Washington	6,613
Connecticut	9,236	Missouri	6,593
Alaska	9,165	South Carolina	6,570
Massachusetts	9,038	Hawaii	6,558
Rhode Island	8,775	Kansas	6,521
Vermont	8,706	Colorado	6,515
Delaware	8,603	Texas	6,460
Pennsylvania	8,191	North Carolina	6,368
Maine	8,178	North Dakota	6,318
Wisconsin	8,158	New Mexico	6,115
Maryland	8,077	Kentucky	6,077
Michigan	8,029	South Dakota	6,063
Wyoming	7,833	Florida	6,020
Illinois	7,585	Oklahoma	6,012
Oregon	7,511	Louisiana	5,934
Ohio	7,499	Arkansas	5,852
West Virginia	7,450	Alabama	5,845
Minnesota	7,447	Nevada	5,778
Indiana	7,287	Tennessee	5,622
Virginia	7,278	Idaho	5,616
New Hampshire	7,065	Mississippi	5,179
California	6,965	Arizona	5,100
Nebraska	6,946	Utah	4,625
Iowa	6,912		
		United States	$ 7,284

Source: Annual Survey of Local Government Finances/U.S. Census Bureau

Spending Note

The above chart is not the final word on spending by the state. Much depends on how "spending" is defined. One study factors in the cost-of-living and for California puts the spending per pupil at $6,258.

Possible Changes

So many people are unhappy with school funding and with the cuts being forced by the deficit, that changes will almost definitely be made in the system. Some possibilities:

- **Categorical Funding, $11 billion.** Where most of the cuts will come. Many politicians, Democrat and Republican, agree that it would be better if some of this money were distributed to the school districts to take care of general expenses, such as salaries and maintenance. As to what programs will be cut? Proably not special education but after that it's anyone's guess. Every program has its champions; arguments will not be lacking.

- **School Allotments.** This is the state money that goes to school districts for salaries and ordinary expenses. Each school is supposed to receive an equal amount, about $4,900 per child. In reality, allotments, according to government reports, range from $4,300 to $8,200 per student. Over the past 40 years, court decisions, legislative action and voter initiatives have made a mishmash of how the schools are funded. With the deficit crisis, equalization will be debated again and chances are that new formulas will be adopted.

- **Minimal Educational Standards.** The courts are hearing a case to require the state to provide a minimal level of funding to all schools. This funding will relieve crowding at schools in poor neighborhoods and improve facilities. Since this suit was filed, many school districts, thanks to changes in the funding laws, have passed improvement bonds. But with the state taking a fresh look at financing, minimal standards may be embraced.

- **Tax Increases.** Governor Schwarzenegger has sworn never, never, but so did Repubicans Ronald Reagan and Pete Wilson and they changed their minds. One possible scenario: lower the approval rate for more taxes from two thirds to 55 percent or 60 percent and allow voters to decide whether to raise taxes.

Good News and Bad

There's no easy way to erase a $38 billion deficit. Even if present funding was maintained, programs would have to be cut. Teachers and classified staffs receive automatic pay increases annually, based on years of service. When these kick in, unless more revenue is provided, school districts will have to make up the money elsewhere and this usually means program cuts.

That's the down side. But there are silver linings:

• California pays its teachers among the tops in the nation. This may slip a bit as the deficit correction takes hold but for at least a few years salaries will remain competitive and districts in need of teachers should have many candidates to choose from.

• After decades of failing to build and renovate schools, voters up and down the state have approved capital improvement bonds. Much of this work is being done now. On the one hand, the schools are starved for cash — operations — on the other, they have relatively plenty — buildings.

• The governor and the legislature are promising to spare the K-12 system as much as they can. Higher education is taking a meaner hit; fees and tuitions have been raised.

• Some programs probably can be cut with little harm. Class sizes in grades K-3 are limited to 20 students. This probably will be raised to 22 or 23.

• Teacher salaries can be reduced, overall, by offering early retirements for veteran teachers (at the top of the scale) and hiring novices (at the bottom of the scale.). Some districts are doing this.

• No one likes to see schools close but money is saved when they are. Because enrollments are declining in many counties, more schools can be closed.

• California has many small school districts. If a fair number consolidated, administrative costs could be reduced.

• There's the state budget and there's the districts' budgets. Local districts can raise their taxes for electives and teachers and operations but they need approval by two-thirds of the voters. This obstacle is hard to overcome but a few districts have. And with the crunch, more districts will try and more will succeed.

The reality, however, is that many parents will be faced with this uncomfortable choice: Put up your own money or your kid's education will suffer. Here are some ways to keep the bill down.

Help on the Cheap

• The metropolitan areas are loaded with academic things to do: museums, planetariums, science and computer centers. Many of them offer programs for the kids. You have to make the effort but the enrichment activities are out there. Buy a local "places to visit, things to do" guide. Or see www.mccormacks.com.

• Community colleges in the summer offer academic camps. Call your local college and see if it has one.

• Cities and recreation districts run summer camps and many offer activity and enrichment classes for the kids during the year. Usually, these agencies mail catalogs to every residence in their jurisdictions but if you don't get one, call city hall.

• Universities offer family camps that mix fun and games with education. Yes, they charge but if you are going to spend the money on a vacation, this might be a reasonable way to keep the family happy and smart.

• Other choices for summer camps: the YMCA.

• Libraries often lack the money to advertise their services but many will have reading programs for the kids. If reading to your nipper is just too much, try the library.

Libraries have free books. Use theirs and avoid the expense of buying books. They have great children's collections and often are open in the evening.

• Web sites. The Web offers a lot of free advice for parents: homework hot lines, reference works, parenting advice. Ask the school or library to recommend some sites or just do a search on parenting or schools.

• Half a loaf. Sometimes, maybe many times, you will be short of time and money and forced to compromise. It's not the end of the world. If you can't afford a professional tutor, settle for a smart college kid or teenager — that sort of thing. Talk to other parents; sometimes they will know about programs and activities that might help your kid.

• Attend the school activities and work with the teacher. According to the studies, these things really do make a big difference.

The Parental Pocket Book

Here's where you, the parent, will either shell out or be asked to. Or where you might decide to shell out.

- **School Associations or Foundations.** Many of them raise funds for class projects and aides. With the state cutbacks, these associations will try to raise more money.

- **Busing.** Many parents want to bring back the Yellow Bus. Cost per student, about $300, with discounts for siblings.

- **School Uniforms.** This might be a money saver. Some schools have dress codes that essentially boil down to sensible clothes for the kids. You have to buy some dark pants and white shirts and plain dresses but you may avoid the fancy and the pricey.

- **Meal tickets.** You can pack the lunch and save but if you want the young mister or miss to dine at school, you're looking at $2 to $3 a day and possibly higher. Many schools use a debit card.

- **Insurance.** $4 to $9 a month per child or $27 for all the children in a family. See Chapter 1, Choosing a School.

- **Photos And Yearbooks.** For photos, depends on the package you want. For yearbooks or Year CDs, maybe $50 to $100.

- **Sports And Extracurricular Activities.** Often the first to go in budget crunches, unless parents ride to the rescue. One high school, struggling to save its $200,000 sports programs, asked parents for donations and help with fund-raisers. To keep football going, each player's family was responsible for raising $859; for girls golf, $429; for boys' basketball, $632.

- **Music instruments.** You have to buy or rent the violin or tuba. Often these can be purchased used.

- **Music and Dance Lessons.** If you want more than the school offers, look in the phone directory under Musical Instruction and Dancing.

- **School outings.** Many times these are funded through the community funds. In the middle grades, many schools fund or used to fund a five-day nature camp in the mountains. If parents are forced to pay the bill, you may be looking at $300 to $400. If you are short of money, the school district might be able to suggest a funding source.

Supplies

Some schools pick up this tab; many don't. About mid summer, Wal-Mart and other stores will set up a kiosk that contains flyers on what the local schools, by grade, are suggesting in the way of supplies. Some samples:

Kindergarten
- Backpack with name
- 1 roll of 24-exposure 35 mm color film
- Colored pencils
- Small bottle of glue or glue sticks
- 4 large glue sticks (nontoxic)
- 64 crayons
- 1 pink eraser with name on it
- 1 box gallon-size zipper-seal freezer bags
- 1 pocket folder
- 1 bottle antibacterial soap
- Supplies will be shared with all the Kindergarten students

First Grade
- Backpack with name
- Crayons
- 4 to 6 glue sticks (nontoxic)
- 2 to 5 #2 pencils sharpened (monthly)
- Large, soft pink eraser
- Small, plastic pencil box and sharpener
- Safety scissors
- Markers
- Up to 2 boxes of facial tissue
- 1 bottle antibacterial soap
- Box of zipper-seal bags (gallon & quart)
- 3 pocket folders

Supplies (Continued)

Second Grade

- Backpack with name
- 2 glue sticks (nontoxic) and 3-ounce bottle of white glue
- 4 #2 lead pencils: (more as needed) and sharpener.
- Erasers and markers
- 1 box unscented face tissues
- 1 folder with two pockets (laminated)
- 1 bottle liquid soap
- Scissors
- Small, plastic pencil box
- Felt-tip markers (wide & fine), nontoxic
- 1 pack AA batteries
- 12-inch ruler with centimeters and inches
- Box of zipper-seal bags (gallon & quart)

Third Grade

- Crayons—16 pack
- Scissors (child size pointed—Fiskars brand)
- 2 Pee-Chee folders
- 5 #2 pencils (more as needed) and sharpener.
- Colored pencils (set of 12)
- Pencil box
- Wide, dry-erase markers
- Box of zipper-seal bags (gallon & quart)
- Felt-tip markers (wide & fine), nontoxic
- Glue sticks and 8-ounce bottle of white glue
- 1 large eraser
- 1 box facial tissues
- 1 red correcting pen
- 1 half-inch thick, 3-hole binder with inside pockets
- 1 highlighter pen

Supplies (Continued)

Fourth Grade

- Small stapler and staples
- Scissors - pointed tip
- 3 Pee-Chee-style folders with three holes
- 8-ounce bottle of white glue or 3 glue sticks
- 1 three-ring, 1-inch binder and binder paper
- 1 smock or large T-shirt
- Crayons
- 5 #2 pencils each month and large eraser
- 1 composition book
- Broad-tip and fine-tip markers
- Colored pencils
- 1 Chapstick (optional)
- 1 book for sustained silent reading (chapter books preferred)
- Book covers for math, science, reading, social studies and language
- 1 box tissues

Fifth and Sixth Grades

- Markers
- Colored pencils
- 8-ounce bottle of white glue
- Binder paper
- Sharpened pencils and sharpener and eraser
- Ruler with metric & standard measures
- 1 protractor
- 1 yellow highlighter
- Assignment notebook (optional)
- Book covers for all texts

The Senior Prom

A dinner dance usually for juniors and seniors and their dates, it is one of the biggest events of a student's school life. There is the excitement of getting dressed up and going out, often in a rented limousine, to a fancy restaurant and then to a dance with a deejay.

Signing Lots Of Blank Checks

For the parents, however, it quickly separates those with platinum credit cards from those with the regular plastic. "You just sign a lot of blank checks," says one mom of three girls. And who do you think will support all those car washes, dinners and coupon book sales the kids staged to fund the prom?

Students plan the prom and hold fund-raisers during the year to defray the costs of tickets (about $50 to $85 each).

Buckboards And Limousines

Cinderella didn't go to the ball in a buckboard and today's kids aren't likely to settle for a Rent-A-Wreck. Limousines generally start at $75 per hour for a sedan (stretch limos are extra) with a six-hour minimum. One limo service offers a prom package of $752 for eight hours. Prices may vary with the number of passengers. Often several couples will share the same limo for economy. The limo driver sometimes functions as a sort of chaperone, which parents like.

One group of seniors beat the limo fees by hiring a taxi for $13 per person.

Tuxedo Under $40? Maybe

A tuxedo can be rented for under $40, but it's more likely you'll pay between $70 and $100. "That's head to toe with a prom discount," says one formal wear agent.

A girl's dress might average about $150 plus another $30 for her shoes.

Don't forget the hair and nails for the girls, about $60 for the perm and another $25 on the manicure. One student reported spending $30 on a manicure and pedicure, which she called a savings.

Wait, There's More!

The prom ticket includes a meal, but many couples feel compelled to dine out at a fancy restaurant as well. And if the kids want to party, they might rent a hotel room. Many parents host the parties themselves to lower their costs and supervise their kids.

Some schools understand that this can be a financial burden and will arrange to buy prom tickets for students who can't afford that cost. The intent is to have every student who wants to, attend the prom.

Flowers And Pictures

Flowers (corsages for the girls, boutonnieres for the boys) have to be bought as well as pictures for each other and the respective families. The starting cost of his boutonniere, usually a rose, ranges from $7 to $10, while her corsage of roses or orchids costs between $20 and $25.

Pictures probably will cost a minimum of $30, if you can get them for that price says one suburban photographer. It's easy for kids to spend $100 on pictures.

The couples often are buying pictures for themselves, their parents and maybe grandparents.

Some good news: the chaperones are free.

Will Grad Nite Be Any Cheaper?

Grad Nite might be cheaper, depending upon the venue. This event is planned and produced by parents with some assistance from the school to assure the grads' safety.

Most Grad Nites are held in the graduates' community, although theme parks such as Disneyland also host the event. Costs range from $50 in some communities to over $125 in others.

Grad Nite is an all-night theme party highly structured with games, dances, music, an abundance of food and nonalcoholic drinks. Once admitted, the grads aren't released except in emergencies and then to their parents. Usually, they gather at the school and are taken en masse to the event. Students should expect that they and their possessions probably will be searched for weapons, drugs and or alcohol.

Another locale popular with the grads, but not necessarily parents, is Mexico.

Why California Sings Money Blues

Income Down (Capital Gains, Stock Options)

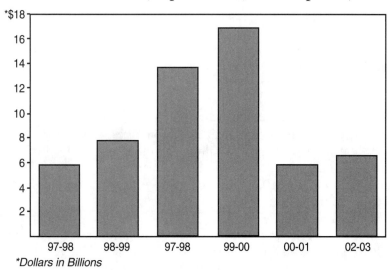

*Dollars in Billions

Expenses Up

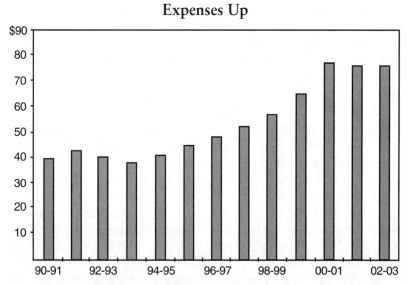

Left Column: Dollars in Billions

Source: California Legislative Analyst Office

11

Sports & Extracurricular

- TYPES OF SPORTS OFFERED
- COMPETETIVE VS. INTRAMURAL
- SCHOLARSHIPS
- COMMUNITY SERVICE
- STUDENT GOVERNMENT

- ELIGIBILITY
- TITLE IX
- CHEERLEADING
- CLUBS

Elementary Grades Overview

Elementary students, on school grounds, play games and exercise under the eye of a physical education instructor and the classroom teacher or yard monitor. The P.E. instructor will have the children do activities to develop their muscles and their coordination.

The elementary students often will get instruction in music and sometimes in art. Not much. School districts typically will assign to three or four schools a music instructor who will visit once or twice a week. The music teacher, for the older students, may organize a band.

Much depends on how much money the school has available for music and the arts.

After school, many students shift to the day-care center, which is stocked with games and offers some activities. Or the kids play games informally on the school grounds.

What the school lacks, parents and private groups provide.

The parent groups run soccer and baseball leagues, Pop Warner football and cheerleading and swimming.

Private firms offer instruction in gymnastics, ballet, dance and acting. Many urban-suburban counties have kids' theater companies.

As for the clubs, there is very little from the school in the elementary years.

About the middle grades, basketball leagues spring into action. Many of them are organized through churches. Indeed, many churches offer a variety of activities for their members.

Another source of activities: sports clubs, notably the family clubs run by the YMCA and the Boys and Girls Clubs.

In the summer, city hall and recreation districts will offer many activities and sports and excursions.

Summing up: a lot to do but little is done at the school.

For information about these activities, you can ask the P.E. coach or city hall or the recreation district. The chamber of commerce may have a list of local clubs.

Or just ask another parent at the school. If you see kids playing soccer and you want your kids to play, stop and talk to the adult in charge.

Check the phone directory under the activity you are interested in.

High School Sports

At the ninth grade, the public schools step up their sports and their activities.

Many high schools will field "school" teams for baseball, soccer, softball, gymnastics, tennis, golf, basketball, volleyball, track, swimming, water polo, diving, wrestling and football. Basketball and the Friday night football games are a popular tradition in many towns and cities.

 Almost all these sports-activities will have teams for boys and girls. Cheerleading is open to boys and girls but is usually more popular with the girls.

Many of these sports are "competitive"— not everyone makes the team, not everyone gets in the game. Adding to the intensity of these contests, players can parlay their skills into college scholarships.

All students still can participate in the P.E. games. .

High School Cultural Activities and Clubs

As organized by the school, they will often include the student newspaper, an arts publication, drama, debate, band, chorus and yearbook.

As organized by students, sometimes with the help of a teacher, clubs can include a great variety: chess, Latin, Spanish, French, Gay, computer, photo, United Nations, environmental, art, etc. Some schools will have many clubs, some schools few.

The school will often list its clubs in the School Accountability Report Card (SARC) or on its Web site.

Clubs typically meet after school and plan their own activities.

Extracurricular Eligibility

To be eligible for many activities, the student must have posted a 2.0 (out of a possible 4.0) grade-point average during the previous quarter and demonstrated progress toward meeting graduating requirements.

Because participation could affect a student's grades, the state lets districts set the bar higher if they wish.

Extracurricular activities are not graded. But many universities give points to students for extra activities and for community service.

Eligibility Sports

Generally, student athletes must be under age 19, enrolled in grades nine through twelve, have a 2.0 average and be declared medically fit, according to the California Interscholastic Federation (CIF) which governs most prep sports programs in the state. This applies to cheerleaders also.

Some schools will bench an athlete whose midterm grades drop below 2.0.

Equipment Or Transportation Fees

Uniforms and equipment are considered property of the districts that, in turn, supply them to the student athletes. The districts pay all transportation costs. They also hire and pay the coaches and other officials. These costs usually are defrayed by ticket and concession sales at the games.

Many districts have established a sports or extracurricular activity participation fee to help defray the costs of providing these programs. In some districts, the fee is voluntary and in others, if you play, you pay. One district sponsors school newspapers. Despite some advertising in the papers, the district charges parents a fee to receive the paper, even if their child is not a member of the staff. Your school should inform you of any and all fees in your enrollment package. If you don't see anything, ask school officials about participation fees.

In some larger schools, during registration, parents run a gantlet of clubs and groups seeking their child's participation and money. This usually is the time when you get the pitch or the bill for your child's P.E., newspaper, yearbook, the parents' booster clubs, the band and several others. Take a checkbook or credit card, find out which fees are mandatory and then decide what else you can afford.

Parents Clubs and Booster Clubs

When money runs short, some activities are quite dependent on the fund-raising efforts of parents. And often this means you reach for your checkbook and write the check.

This holds for band and other extracurricular activities and for sports. Some of the sports teams, particularly basketball and football, will have booster clubs. These clubs raise money for equipment, uniforms, plaques, trophies and the like. They often include local business people who, out of civic pride and maybe some mercantilism, wish to support the teams.

Many parents volunteer for the snack shack, a steady moneymaker for schools.

Coaches

Larger schools may hire an athletic director who selects the various coaches with backgrounds both in physical education and athletics. State law requires that coaches and referees be trained in the rules of the sport and how to teach it. California Interscholastic Federation (CIF) training includes the rules and philosophy of the sport, along with information about sexual harassment and sportsmanship. Just as teachers are required to remain current in their fields, so too are coaches and referees.

Usually coaches are teachers trained by the CIF and paid by the district. The pay varies with each district's contract with the teachers' union. (See pay in Chapter 3, Teachers).

Insurance

School district insurance covers student athletes, although supplemental insurance is available to those who request it.

Title IX

Title IX, enacted in 1973, is intended to increase athletic opportunities for girls and women. All education programs receiving federal money are supposed to comply with the law. It doesn't mean coed wrestling or football, but it does say that school girls and college women should have the same opportunities to participate in sports as do boys and men.

If your daughter is interested in sports, check with your school and find out what programs are available and how her opportunities to participate compare with those of boys. Universities used to limit their sports scholarships to boys; now many go to girls.

P.E. Requirements

A student must complete two years to graduate. Some high schools allow students to count driver's education toward the P.E. requirement.

Showers After P.E.

Because time is short, students usually skip shower for the intramural sports, except maybe for swimming (get the chlorine out of the hair). Elementary and middle schools rarely have shower facilities. After high-school sports, showers are up to the students.

P.E. Uniforms

Depending on the class your child is taking, a uniform might be required. Some schools simply say go buy a certain color pair of shorts etc. while others require a shirt and shorts of the school's color bearing the school logo. All schools require athletic shoes with the style and color varying. Writing a check to the school or the sporting goods store is almost inevitable.

Faculty Advisors

Depending upon their union's contract with the district, teachers may be assigned or volunteer to be club advisors according to their interests.

Religious Groups

Students may organize religious meetings as a group, as long as the meetings do not interfere with their classes and the school is not involved in any religious indoctrination.

Community Use Of Schools

Schools often are used as community meeting places to discuss and consider various public issues such as education, recreation, science, community development. Child care facilities often operate at school sites as do youth groups such as Boy Scouts, Girl Scouts, Camp Fire Girls and others. As in other states, schools serve as emergency shelters during natural disasters in California. Where the law draws the line: you can't rent a school for a rally to overthrow the government.

Districts may charge a fee for the use, but the fee must be only for the district's direct costs such as cleaning and utilities.

Religious groups also may use school facilities. They, too, must pay any fees.

Student Government

Most middle and high schools have some form of student government where students elect representatives to establish rules and to run student-financed events and programs at the school. Some schools require membership in a leadership class and at least a 2.0 grade-point average (out of a possible 4.0) or better.

Junior ROTC

Many California schools offer a Junior Reserve Officers Training Corps program run by one of the services: Navy, Air Force or Army. Students participating in this voluntary program get an overview of military duties and responsibilities as well as training in leadership and citizenship.

> ### T-P, a California tradition
> *Your son or daughter joins a school team and it wins a few games or the cheerleaders win some prize — any excuse will do — and some parent will drive the kids around and they will fling toilet paper over your house, car, trees and shrubs. Damn nuisance but the kids love it.*

Yearbooks Aren't Books Anymore

Your old high school yearbooks are sitting on the bookshelf where your kids can pull them down and laugh at what was cool then. But your kids may have to pop their "yearbooks" into the DVD player if they want to check out some old lost flame.

No longer will kids be able to write over unflattering pictures. Now they can have them digitally enhanced, hear interviews or personal recollections of the school year.

Most students are still opting for the cheaper printed books, but the future is here and it is digital. Discs are more versatile, have more space and take up less room on the bookshelf.

Homecoming

Homecoming is one of the biggest social events of the school year, ranking up there with graduation and the senior prom.

It is an elaborate ritual that has grown into a full week of activities known as "Spirit Week." The students build floats, which are usually featured in a town parade, generally held on Friday afternoon.

On Friday night, to the cheers of thousands of students, parents and alumni, the football team takes to the field for the Big Game. At half time, the Homecoming queen and king are crowned. After the game, the alumni chat with friends and former teachers and the students take off to the gym for the Homecoming Dance.

Where There's A Will...

School administrators say that the more parents are involved in their children's education, the more the kids benefit. For example:

One group of parents, frustrated by a decade of waiting for a pool to be restored to service, decided not to wait any longer. The parents got it reopened by persuading other community agencies to contribute toward the $165,000 repair tab.

In another community, one parent, an attorney, volunteered to sponsor the school's debate team.

Many Silicon Valley-area schools owe their high-tech prowess to the talents of parents who donated time, money and equipment.

12

Schedules & Busing

- **TYPICAL DAILY SCHEDULE**
- **YEAR-ROUND SCHEDULE**
- **PICK UP AND DROP OFF**
- **TYPICAL SCHOOL YEAR**
- **HOLIDAYS**
- **BUSING**

Getting to school on time and navigating a school year can be a bit confusing.

Many schools don't follow traditional schedules. And even when they do, you will often find little surprises, such as half days and unexpected holidays (that might send you scrambling for day care). Let's begin with the most popular annual schedule.

Typical Schedule

- School starts in late August or early September and breaks for Easter and Christmas-New Year's Day and goes on vacation in early June.
- Instruction is spread out over 180 teaching days.
- School starts at about 8 a.m. and lets out about 2 p.m. or 2:30 p.m.
- Kindergarten students attend half-day sessions, about four hours, but a campaign is underway to increase the hours to six. About 35 school districts in the state are offering full-day (six hours) kindergartens for at least some of their children.

Not Chiseled In Stone

At many schools this schedule is more a guide than a rule.

The state, in many instances, defines attendance by hours not days.

Schools are required to provide a minimum of:

- 600 hours in kindergarten.
- 840 hours in grades one through three .
- 900 hours in grades four through eight.
- 1,080 hours in grades nine through twelve.

Some Things Affecting Schedules.

- Year-round schools
- Parent-teacher conferences
- Training days
- Holidays and special events such as Easter Holidays, Spring Break, Ski Week, etc.
- Weather or natural disasters.

Don't Stress, Get Organized

Experts advise that some planning and organization can help families avoid school morning stress:

- *Don't do in the morning what you can do the night before. Clear the dinner dishes and replace them with break-fast dishes. Put all books, papers and projects in an easily accessible place where they can be picked up quickly as you leave in the morning.*
- *Make a family calendar or daily agenda list and put it where everyone will see it — maybe next to the phone, on the bulletin board or refrigerator. List all daily events and tasks, including school work, no matter how ordinary.*
- *Reserve time each evening for homework. Make yourself available to help. Phone calls can be returned after home-work.*
- *All those emergency notification and parental release or consent forms the school sends you— photocopy them so you don't have to spend time filling them out each time the need arises.*
- *Postpone volunteer work for a few years or maye 12 years. Spend that time on your kids and their schooling.*

What is a typical school year?

A regular school year typically runs from late August to early or mid-June. The schedule often will look like this.

August
25- 26 – Orientation for New Teachers
27 - 28 – Teacher Work Days

September
1 - Labor Day – No School
2 - Work Day – All Teachers
3 - Classes Begin – First Day of School

October
No Holidays
31 - End of First Quarter*

November
11 - Veteran's Day – No School
25 - End of First Trimester*
26 - Thanksgiving Recess – No School
27 - Thanksgiving Day – No School
28 - Thanksgiving Recess – No School

December
22 - January 2 – Winter Recess - No School

January
1 - New Year's Day – No School
5 - School Starts
19 - Dr. Martin Luther King's Day – No School
30 - End of First Semester*

February
9 - Lincoln's Day – No School
16 - Washington's Day - No School. (Note: Some districts combine the holidays and add a few more holidays to create a "ski week." The days are made up later.)

March
19 - End of Second Trimester*

April
2 - End of Third Quarter*
12 - 16 – Spring Recess

May
31 - Memorial Day – No School

June
11 - Last Day of School
11 - End of Third Trimester, Fourth Quarter, and Second Semester Report cards usually come out at the end of the quarter, semester or trimester.

Which holidays do public schools observe?

Public schools close for New Year's Day, Martin Luther King Day (usually the third Monday in January or a Monday or Friday in the week of January 15), Lincoln's Day (usually the Monday or Friday in the week of Feb. 12), Washington's Day (the third Monday in February), Memorial Day, July 4, Labor Day, Veteran's Day, Thanksgiving and Christmas.

Some districts also observe Caesar Chavez's birthday on March 31 or Native-American Day on the fourth Friday in September or Columbus Day (October).

All schools close for one week in spring around Easter, either before or after Easter. Some districts call it Spring Vacation or Spring Break. Districts also may close for other holidays declared at their discretion such as Columbus Day, Fourth of July (summer school), Admission Day, etc.

Many parents who are not Christian and whose religious holidays are not observed by local schools keep their children home, sending a note to excuse the absence.

Year-round Schools

Short of money after 1970, California structured funding to reward schools that went to all-year calendars. Schedules divide the year into four periods called tracks. Students attend school for three of the four tracks. This calendar was taken from a district that has used the year-round approach for many years. Because high school students have activities that mesh with the regular calendar, high schools shy away from the year-round approach.

Regular holidays were observed. The Christmas break went from Dec. 24 to Jan. 2. There was no spring or Easter break.

All schools in the district were closed from July 1 to July 24.

To make up time, this district turned 10 minimum days into full instructional days and added 6-9 minutes to the school day.

Track A

- First Day of first session, Monday, Aug. 18
- End of first session, Oct. 31
- Break, Nov. 1 to Dec. 8.
- First day, second session, Dec. 8
- End of second session, March 15
- Break, March 16 to April 12.
- First day, third session, April 12
- Last day of school, June 30

Track B.

- First Day of first session, Thursday, July 24
- End of first session, Aug. 15
- Break, Aug. 15 to Sept. 15
- First day, second session, Sept. 15
- End of second session, Dec. 5
- Break, Dec. 5 to Jan. 20
- First day, third session, Jan. 20
- End of third session, April 9
- Break, April 9 to May 4.
- First day, fourth session, May 4
- Last day of school, June 30

Track C

• First Day of first session, Thursday, July 24
• End of first session, Sept. 12
• Break, Sept. 12 to Oct. 13
• First day, second session, Oct. 13
• End of second session, Jan. 16
• Break, Jan. 16 to Feb. 17
• First day, third session, Feb. 17
• End of third session, May 3
• Break, May 3 to June 1
• First day, fourth session, June 1
• Last day of school, June 30

Track D

• First Day of first session, July 24
• End of first session, Oct. 10
• Break, Oct. 10 to Nov. 3
• First day, second session, Nov. 3
• End of second session, Feb. 13
• Break, Feb. 13 to March 16
• First day, third session, March 16
• Last day of school, May 28

Complaints About Year-round Schooling

If you have several children and one is attending a year-round school and another a school with a traditional calendar, you may find the schedules hard to reconcile.

Year-round often interferes with summer vacations and with parental work schedules.

In some districts, parents try to get the jump on registration to secure the more favorable tracks. This sometimes leads to hard feelings among those who missed out.

Teacher Training Day

Just what it says: days off so teachers can do training. Most teachers are required to take skill classes covering 150 hours over five years or about 30 hours a year. In the 1990s, training days were common; then some were given up to extend instructional days to 180.

Some districts may not have training days or they may be scheduled before the start of the school year.

Check the calendar.

Weather Days

The song says, "It Never Rains in California."

Wrong. It does and, in some regions, when it rains it floods, washing out roads and causing detours. Schools are closed, generally for no more than a day, and the closure is announced on local radio and television.

Schools above the snow line will close or operate on a shorter schedule some days when snows make roads impassable and schools inaccessible.

Schools make up the lost time by tacking days onto the end of the school year or by adding hours here and there.

Fog is a factor in some Central Valley districts. The California Highway Patrol won't let school buses run when drivers say they can't see objects at least 200 feet away. Each district has its own procedures for dealing with bad weather. Ask your child's school for its weather policy.

During severe weather, call the school to determine if it is open.

Saturday School

Saturday school is a remedial program for students in danger of repeating the same grade or dropping out.

It also targets students with disciplinary as well as academic problems, offering them supplemental instruction and some punishment. "We may pick up trash half the day and hit the books the other half," one administrator said.

Summer School

This is another exception to the 180-day school year.

Summer school is voluntary. The six-week program allows students lacking enough credits to graduate on time to take courses aimed at getting them caught up. Students don't spend as many hours per day in class because they are not taking as many classes as they would in a regular session. If your child has failed or is falling behind, discuss summer school with your local school.

Camp Break

About the sixth grade, many school districts drive the kids into the mountains for a week-long nature or science camp.

Almost every county is located within one or two hours of a mountainous region, even if the mountains rise only to 2,000 or so feet. Many camps have been set up in these areas.

Schools contract with the camps to give the kids a firsthand look at nature and to do science experiments. And to get out of school and have some fun and do something new. Fun mixed with learning. Teachers and parental chaperones tag along.

You have to give your permission with a signed form. And you may have to pay for meals, buses and camp costs. If you are short of funds, talk to the teacher. The schools will distribute a flier about the camp. For more information, talk to the teacher.

For memories, send along a cheap, easy-to-use camera.

Holidays South of the Border

Many families, particularly in Southern California, visit relatives in Mexico during the Christmas holidays. The children go too, often for a month, disrupting their schooling in California.

To cope with this, some districts have modified their calendars or placed the students on an independent study program while they're in Mexico. Others are adamant about students returning on time after the two-week holiday break.

Some districts drop students from their enrollment, a move that has prompted many families to abbreviate their holidays. Before making any plans for an extended Christmas in Mexico or elsewhere with the children, contact their schools about their holiday absence policies.

Ski Week

Also called winter break (around Easter comes spring break). California has some great ski resorts. Some school districts take the presidential holidays and throw in a few more days and come up with a ski week, usually in February. The lost days are made up later. Some people look upon ski week as a shameful California indulgence. Our advice: Chill out, Dude!

Minimum Day

A "minimum day," is a shorter school day than normal. Often during testing and parent-teacher conferences and other occasions, students are released early. These dates are posted on the school calendar and notices usually are sent to the parents. Check your school for a list of minimum days so you can arrange for day care or transportation if necessary.

20 Largest School Districts

District	County	Enrollment
1 Los Angeles USD*	Los Angeles	746,852
2 San Diego City USD	San Diego	140,753
3 Long Beach USD	Los Angeles	97,212
4 Fresno USD	Fresno	81,222
5 Santa Ana USD	Orange	63,610
6 San Francisco USD	San Francisco	58,216
7 San Bernardino USD	San Bernardino	56,096
8 Sacramento City USD	Sacramento	52,850
9 Oakland USD	Alameda	52,501
10 Elk Grove USD	Sacramento	52,418
11 San Juan USD	Sacramento	52,212
12 Garden Grove USD	Sacramento	50,066
13 Capistrano USD	Orange	48,608
14 Corona-Norco USD	Riverside	41,977
15 Riverside USD	Riverside	40,888
16 Fontana USD	San Bernardino	40,168
17 Stockton USD	San Joaquin	39,421
18 Sweetwater Union High	San Diego	37,878
19 Mt. Diablo USD	Contra Costa	36,891
20 Montebello USD	Los Angeles	35,590

Source: California Department of Education, 2002-2003. K-12 Enrollment.
*USD stands for unified school district.

Enrollment, Fall 2002-03

Rank	State	Total
1	California	6,244,403
2	Texas	4,223,192
3	New York	2,845,000
4	Florida	2,533,628
5	Illinois	2,089,633
6	Pennsylvania	1,816,747
7	Ohio	1,813,411
8	Michigan	1,744,940
9	Georgia	1,496,012
10	New Jersey	1,367,222
11	North Carolina	1,345,889
12	Virginia	1,176,557
13	Washington	1,015,968
14	Indiana	995,195
15	Massachusetts	987,986
16	Arizona	940,433
17	Tennessee	910,364
18	Missouri	894,029
19	Wisconsin	881,231
20	Maryland	866,743
21	Minnesota	846,891
22	Colorado	751,862
23	Louisiana	729,516
24	Alabama	721,633
25	South Carolina	672,224
26	Kentucky	629,020
27	Oklahoma	624,202
28	Connecticut	571,890
29	Oregon	553,115
30	Mississippi	491,623
31	Iowa	482,210
32	Utah	481,143
33	Kansas	469,634
34	Arkansas	445,229
35	Nevada	369,498
36	New Mexico	320,034
37	Nebraska	283,930
38	West Virginia	281,591
39	Idaho	248,515
40	New Hampshire	207,628
41	Maine	204,337
42	Hawaii	183,829
43	Rhode Island	157,996
44	Montana	149,995
45	Alaska	134,364
46	South Dakota	124,988
47	Delaware	116,274
48	North Dakota	103,013
49	Vermont	99,657
50	Wyoming	86,117
51	Washington D.C.	67,522
	U.S.A.	47,798,062

Source: National Education Association, August 2003

Nothing Hidden

School districts want you to know what's coming. They don't want to surprise you (which would generate many complaints). They publish their schedules before the start of the school year. They mail them to parents in the district.

If you are shopping for a home, get the schedule straight off. The year-round schools may really challenge your job schedule.

A word of advice from parents (the authors) who have gotten the schedule in the mail and said, "Another piece of paper. Who needs this? "

And chucked it into the garbage.

Big mistake! You forget the minimum days, the training days and sometimes the holidays. Then you have to scramble for child care. Good idea: Tack the schedule onto kitchen wall or bulletin board.

A Typical Schedule

A typical elementary schedule might start at 8:05 a.m., break for lunch at 11:25 a.m. and dismiss at 2:45 p.m. Elementary students in grades 1-3 might start at 8:15 a.m., break for lunch around 11:25 a.m. and dismiss at 2:35 p.m. Upper grades would follow the same schedule and be dismissed at 2:40 p.m.

High-school students might start as early as 7:30 a.m., breaking for lunch around 12:30 p.m. and being dismissed around 2:45 p.m. Others start around 8:05 a.m and dismiss at 3:15 p.m. For example, a student might have history at 8:05 a.m. on Monday and get out later than on Tuesday when she has biology which starts at 7:30 a.m.

Some high schools try to load ninth-, tenth- and eleventh-graders with seven periods daily so they will have fewer classes in their senior year and be able to leave early. That policy is not popular with students who have jobs or are trying to get to sports events.

Always there are exceptions. One Southern California high school, to relieve crowding, offered voluntary classes starting at 6:24 a.m with dismissal before 1 p.m. "It benefits the kids who have got to work after school," said the assistant principal.

Kindergarten

Kindergarten usually is offered from around 8 a.m. to 11:30 a.m. Some schools, however, also offer a second or afternoon session running from about 11:30 a.m. until 3 p.m. Some schools offer full-day kindergarten. Ask for a copy of the bell schedule so you will know what time your child must be at school and when he will be dismissed.

Block Schedules

Although its value is debated by academics, block scheduling is practiced at many high schools and some middle schools and junior highs. The idea is to allow students to work on certain subjects for longer periods and to eliminate some of the interruptions in the normal school day. In a typical arrangement, the first period runs 50 minutes and the other periods run 95 minutes.

On the first day, a student with a seven-period schedule might attend science, English, foreign language, history. On the alternate day, science, math, physical education, drama. Some days are longer than others. Actual practice varies by school and student.

A typical "short" day might look like:

7:29 a.m. Bell rings. Six minutes to get to class.

7:35 to 8:25 a.m. First period, 50 minutes.

8:25 a.m. Bell rings. Six minutes to get to next class.

8:31 a.m. to 10:06 a.m. Second subject, 95 minutes.

10:06 to 10:16 a.m. Long passing (snacks), 10 minutes.

10:16 a.m. Bell rings. Six minutes to get to class.

10:22 a.m. to 11:57 a.m. Third subject, 95 minutes.

11:57 a.m. Bell rings.

11:57 a.m. to 12:27 p.m. Lunch, 30 minutes.

12:27 p.m. Bell rings. Six minutes to get to next class.

12:33 p.m. to 2:08 p.m. Fourth subject, 95 minutes.

2:08 p.m. Bell rings, school dismissed.

Fifth-Grade Schedule
(from interview with fifth-grade teacher)

8:25 a.m. Bell goes off. Students go to class, unload backpacks outside door, leave them outside, bring class materials inside. Teachers takes roll call by silently noting who's absent. Teacher occasionally reads announcement from principal's office; most announcements are sent home in bulletin.

8:25 a.m. to 9 a.m. Language activity. Write in journal. Teacher puts sentences on board or overhead screen; students edit them. Class might go over homework with teacher. Students read aloud or teacher reads.

9 a.m. to 10:25 a.m. Language arts. Each week the pupils read a story from an anthology. Spelling and grammar. One major writing project a month; example, a favorite place. The project often takes several drafts. Before school started, fifth grade teachers met and decided on anthology and on lesson plans. These plans tie into the state curriculum. Teacher works off of lesson plan to cover material.

10:25 a.m. to 10:45 a.m. 20-minute recess. Bathrooms, play. Teachers take 10-minute break; rotate through yard duty.

10:45 a.m. Math warm-up, 15 minutes. Teacher reviews what has been covered.

11 a.m. to 11:40 a.m. Math project for day. One example, use cups of jelly beans to illustrate probability — how many reds, pinks, etc. This teacher tests students before tackling a subject. If students pass with 85 percent, she lets them work on another math project while she works with the rest of the class. Gifted students (high achieving) also receive special work. Students with learning disabilities may be pulled out of class for short periods of instruction.

11:40 a.m. to 12:25 p.m. Social studies, U.S. history. The daily schedule is posted in the class so students know what's next. Read from texts and take notes. Possible class project: life in colonial days. Students might create a mock-up of a colonial fort or write a journal of life on the Mayflower.

(Fifth-Grade Schedule cont.)

12:25 p.m. to 1 p.m. Lunch 35 minutes. Students line up and walk to cafeteria. Sit at assigned tables. Teacher also takes a 35-minute lunch break. When students finish, they go outside and play. Two monitors (nonteachers) in cafeteria, two in yard. Lunch is served at staggered times; some kids eat earlier and return to class earlier. Each group has a different bell sound. At 1 p.m., bell ring s for this group and they return to class.

1 p.m. to 2 p.m. Physical Education (P.E.) two days a week. On one day, the class will be run by credentialed P.E. teacher (from district office). Class runs a mile, does activities to develop specific motor skills, stretching, exercising, etc. Second day, the class is run by the teacher who breaks students into teams for games. Different game each week, soccer, football, basketball, etc.

2 p.m. to 2:30 p.m. On P.E. days, silent reading.

2:30 p.m. to 2:50 p.m. Literature. Read assigned books. Discuss in class.

1 p.m. to 1:30 p.m. On days when there is no P.E., kids do silent reading. Teacher circulates in class, helping individuals or small groups.

1:30 p.m. to 2:20 p.m. On days when there is no P.E., science for 30-40 minutes. Class gets science three days a week, on days when there is no P.E.

2:10 p.m. to 2:50 p.m. On days when there is no P.E., literature.

2:50 p.m. Copy homework assignment. Teacher answers questions about assignment. Clean up desks and around desks.

3:05 p.m. Class dismissed.

DARE officer comes in one morning a week to discourage kids from using drugs.

Half hour of music or library once a week in mornings.

Teacher must be at school be 7:55 a.m. This teacher corrects papers and sees parents after school. Usually leaves about 5 p.m.

Typical Schedule
(interview with sixth-grade, middle school teacher)

8:25 a.m. Bell rings, informing students that they have two minutes to get to class.

8:27 a.m. Bell rings again. Students should be in homeroom class.

8:25 a.m. to 8:45 a.m. Silent reading. School announcements read over public address system by members of the school leadership council (students). Pledge of allegiance.

8:45 a.m. Bell rings. Five minutes to get to next class.

8:50 a.m. Math class. 50 minutes.

9:40 a.m. Bell rings, five minutes to get to next class.

9:45 a.m. Physical Education. 50 minutes. Intramural games, exercise. Might dismiss a little early to allow students to get ready for next period.

10:35 a.m. Bell rings, five minutes to get to next class.

10:40 a.m. Science class, 50 minutes.

11:30 a.m. Bell rings, lunch.

11:30 a.m. Lunch, 30 minutes. Students walk to lunch room on their own. Can buy food at snack bar or go through cafeteria line. Or eat own lunch.

12:00 p.m. Bell rings. Five minutes to get to next class.

12:05 p.m. English, 50 minutes.

12:55 p.m. Bell rings. Five minutes to get to next class.

1 p.m. History, 50 minutes.

1:50 p.m. Bell rings. Five minutes to get to next class.

1:55 p.m. Electives. 50 minutes. Band, choir, orchestra, student leadership, yearbook, computers.

2:45 p.m. Bell rings. School dismissed.

- Afterschool sports. One organized sport, basketball, for boys and girls.
- Afterschool academics. Help with homework. Opportunity to review what was taught in class.

Typical Schedule
Twelfth Grade, High School (Student interview)

7:29 a.m. Bell rings. Students have six minutes to get to class.

7:35 a.m. to 8:25 a.m. Bell rings again. Science class, 50 minutes.

8:25 a.m. Bell rings. Six minutes to get to next class.

8:31 to 9:24 a.m. English. Daily announcements read over intercom. 53 minutes including 3 minutes for bulletin.

9:24 a.m. Bell rings. Six minutes to get to next class.

9:30 a.m. to 10:20 a.m. Mathematics, 50 minutes.

10:20 a.m. Bell rings, class over.

10:20 a.m. to 10:30 a.m. "Long passing" or brunch. Students may purchase breakfast foods a la carte.

10:30 a.m. Bell rings. Six minutes to get to next class.

10:36 a.m. to 11:26 a.m. Foreign language, 50 minutes.

11:26 a.m. Bell rings. Six minutes to get to next class.

11:32 a.m. to 12:22 p.m. Physical education. Team or individual sports offered. 50 minutes.

12:22 p.m. Bell rings.

12:22 p.m. to 12:53 p.m. Lunch. Students may purchase food from cafeteria or eat food brought from home. 31 minutes.

12:53 p.m. Lunch over. Six minutes to get to next class.

12:59 p.m. to 1:49 p.m. History, 50 minutes.

1:49 p.m. Bell rings. School is over, unless student has a seventh period.

1:55 p.m. to 2:45 p.m. Electives. Drama, art, leadership. 50 minutes.

2:45 p.m. Bell rings. School is dismissed.

Busing

After Prop. 13 cut state taxes in 1978, almost all school districts dropped school busing. Among the 50 states, California ranks at the bottom in the yellow bus (the school bus).

Busing was retained for sporting and special events, for disabled children and for hardship cases. Crowded schools sometimes use the yellow bus to transport students assigned to alternate schools. Some magnet schools, to encourage transfers, provide free busing.

In the 1990s, at the behest of parents, some school districts brought back the yellow bus and charged the parents for the cost, about $300 a child with possible discounts for siblings.

More districts are thinking about bringing back the yellow buses. It's not just convenience; it's also safety.

Public transit agencies have filled some of the need. Many agencies coordinate their schedules to have buses swing by as school lets out. It varies from town to town. In the big cities, the transit agencies will often have multiple buses sitting right outside the schools when they let out. Other agencies run the buses close to the schools.

Also in big cities, trains, trolleys and light rail carry students. Many of these agencies will sell a discount ticket to students.

Unlike school buses, public transit can evict an unruly or rowdy passenger anywhere along the route.

Stopping For School Buses

Whether you are approaching or following a school bus, stop when you see the red lights flashing on the bus. Those lights mean the driver has stopped to let students get on or off. Children don't always stop to look for cars before dashing across the road after exiting a school bus, thus the requirement. Failure to stop can result in a heavy fine.

Traffic approaching a bus on the opposite side of a divided highway is exempt from stopping.

Seat Belts On Buses

By 2005, new school buses carrying 16 or more passengers will be equipped with "three-point" seat belts like those in your car. Existing buses, however, will be exempt.

Bus Driver Training

All drivers must have a special certificate issued only after completing 40 hours of instruction: 20 in the classroom and 20 more behind the wheel in an actual school bus. Drivers must pass a physical every time they renew their license and must be fingerprinted by the California Highway Patrol. Additionally, every school bus maintenance facility in the state is inspected every 13 months for any safety violations.

Alternatives

The most popular is the car; you drive your kids to school. Or you share the job with other parents.

Many kids walk or take their bicycles. Many cities and suburban towns have striped their streets for bicycle lanes. The kids often ignore the lanes and use the sidewalks.

Another alternative: skateboards.

Comments from Kindergarten Teachers

• *Many parents are nervous that their children will be nervous. They ask me, what do I need to know and how do I prepare. They want to know if the classroom has a bathroom. I tell them to visit the classroom and see what we do. And to make the kindergarten orientation meeting. Also to volunteer, if they can. Many parents are willing to do things at home.*

• *For the first days, we try to have fun and put the children at ease. Books and puppets and toys, a playhouse, "cubbies" where the children can gather and get to know each other. We have parent volunteers and sometimes extra help.*

• *It's important for parents to trust teachers. If they have concerns, talk to us. Keep the lines of communication open.*

• *The most important thing: read to your child every night.*

• *We get a real array of children, the ready and the not ready. We divide children into groups according to needs.*

• *Parents should try to get their children to share and take turns and to talk and use words.*

• *Children need sleep. Try to get them to bed by 8.*

13

Healthy, Well-fed and Safe

- SCHOOL FOOD, MENUS
- P.E. AND FITNESS
- HEALTH AND INSURANCE
- SCHOOL SAFETY
- WHEN YOUR CHILD IS SICK OR HURT

- NUTRITION
- IMMUNIZATIONS
- MEDICINE
- EARTHQUAKE , FIRE

The Skinny On Fat

Kids like fat. It's unfortunate, it's deplorable, it's unhealthy. It's true.

California school menus are created by dieticians. Many of the items they choose are healthy and nutritious. Go to any school lunchroom and you will almost always find bananas, apples, yogurt, lettuce, fruit drinks, milk, veggie burgers, tuna sandwiches, the makings of salad and, at the larger schools, vegetarian meals.

If you want your child to eat healthy, he can — if he chooses. Some do; many, many don't.

Several years ago, Berkeley High School commissioned Alice Waters, creator of California cuisine, to devise nutritious and tasty choices.

The students sipped, chewed, swallowed and gave the verdict, "No thanks!"

Schools concede this reality by providing what the kids crave: burgers, hot dogs, pizza, fries, nachos, burritos and sugary snacks. Loads of fat and sugar.

So ingrained are these cravings, so fiercely ignorant are the students — said one young scholar, "A nice sugar buzz never hurt anyone." — that many an adult is tempted to take the old "good-for-you" cook book and chuck it into the Pacific.

But brave hearts carry on and people are starting to listen, especially since obesity and diabetes have been identified as major problems and also since more has become known about those clever people in the food game. When old fat became too costly, they came up with trans fat, which excels at clogging arteries but is cheaper.

Running Battle

What has come to pass is a running battle where parents and dieticians pressure the schools to encourage the kids to switch to the healthy and tell the food and drink sellers to back off on the student market. Some examples:

• Several years ago, up and down the state, sugar-water purveyors, including Coca-Cola and Pepsi, went to school districts and cooed, let us put our soda machines on campus and we will give you a cut of the take.

Many districts, short of money, said, "Welcome aboard!"

Parents lit into the districts and into the politicians to get rid of the machines. In 2003, the legislature banned the sale of soft drinks in elementary and middle schools; this law will take effect in 2005. Although students may bring sodas from home, they won't be able to buy them at school except during school activities or fund-raisers that begin 30 minutes after school.

Additionally, any district considering a soda machine contract must hold a public hearing on the issue. High schools were exempted from the ban but the writing is on the wall: Controls are coming.

• Many schools sell brand-name fast food — Pizza Hut, Taco Bell, Burger King, etc. — but the purveyors must lower the fat:
   - Calories from fat ratio must be 35 percent or less
   - No more than 10 percent of all calories from saturated fat.
   - Sugar cannot exceed 35 percent of total weight, except for fruit and vegetables.

• More milk, fruit juice and water are being stocked in vending machines

• More encouragement is being given to meals featuring fruit, vegetables and snacks such as yogurt, fruit or granola.

Sample Menus

Breakfast

Mon.	Tues.	Wed.	Thurs.	Fri.
Cinn. Roll Cereal Cheese Stick Fruit Juice Milk	Breakfast Burrito Cereal Bear Grahams Fruit Juice Milk	Giant Muffin Cereal Jungle Crackers Fruit Juice Milk	Cinn. Texas Toast Cereal Strawberry Yogurt Fruit Juice Milk	Cheese Bread Cereal Sunflwr. Seeds Fruit Juice Milk
Pears Bagel Milk	Fresh Orange Muffin Tops Milk Raisins Milk	Orange Juice Fruit Yogurt Honey Toast Milk	Wildberry Juice Waffle Sticks Raisins Milk	Applesauce Donut Cereal
Super Bun Fruit Milk	French Toast Peaches Milk	Egg Burrito Fresh Orange Milk	Pancake Applesauce Milk	Pizza Bagel Fruit Milk
Juice Cereal Grahams Milk	Apple Juice Pop Tart String Cheese Milk	Grape Juice Pancake Sausage Milk	Orange Juice Cinnamon Roll Milk	Fruit Punch Sausage & Cheese Sandwich Milk
Cereal Muffin Fruit Milk	Strwbrry Poptart Chilled Fruit Grahams Milk	Break. Burrito Chilled Fruit Milk	French Toast w/ syrup Chilled Fruit Milk	Cinn. Bun Chilled Fruit Milk

Lunch

Mon.	Tues.	Wed.	Thurs.	Fri.
Chick. Nuggets Potato Wedges Green Beans Fruit Milk	Spaghetti Deluxe Salad French Bread Fruit Milk	Hot Dog Veg. Beans Baby Carrots Fruit Ice Fruit Milk	Teriyaki Beef Steamy Rice Mixed Veg. Cookie Fruit Milk	Cheese Pizza Corn Baby Carrots Fruit Milk
Corn Dog Enchirito Fresh Apple Milk Raisins	Chick. Nuggets Veggie Burger Green Beans Jicama Chocolate Milk Dried Fruit	Burrito Fresh Fruit Celery Sticks Milk Raisins	Lemon Chick. Veggie Dog Carrot Sticks Pears Milk Raisins	Nachos Chick. Sand. Fresh Fruit Milk
Chick. Nuggets French Bread Tater Rounds Fruit Cup Juice Milk Catsup	Beef Taquitos Spanish Rice Apple Fresh Salsa Juice Milk	Classic Burger Hamburger Lettuce Banana Juice Milk Catsup	Spaghetti French Bread Pineapple Juice Milk	Cheese Pizza Salad Fresh Pear Fruit Snack Juice Milk
Cosmic Caesar Wet Burrito Chick. Nuggets Tuna Salad Yogurt Parfait Egg Salad Sand. Roast Beef	BLT Salad Pasta Bowl Monterey Ranch Sandwich Chili Burrito Fresh Turkey	Chick. Salad Spicy Chicken Wet Burrito Chick. on Bun Tuna Sandwich Egg Salad Sand.	Cosmic Caesar Hot Dog Caesar Wrap Burrito Nachos Tuna Sand.	Spinach Salad Calzone Rice Bowl Chick.Tenders Chili Burrito Fresh Sub
Hamburger Tater Tots Mand. Orange Banana Chips	Chili & Cheese Tossed Salad Pears Grammy Bears	Chick. Nuggets Potato Wedges Grapes Peaches	Baked Ham Potatoes Veggie Sticks Choc. Milk	Pizza Mixed Veg. Applesauce

The Future

Kiddie dining is heating up to be one of those crusades that catch the interest of Americans, particularly Californians. Think of smoking and cigarettes and you have some idea of what's coming, except it probably won't be as intense.

Obesity has been identified as a major health threat; diabetes is afflicting more children and adults.

You can argue that adults are responsible for their own choices but with kids the feeling is taking hold that more has to be done to shield them from the fat and sugar merchants and nudge them toward healthier foods.

Parents Can Influence The Menu

Parents can make their opinions known about the food, either to the principal and cafeteria supervisor or to the school board. If it's a matter of a special dietary need, some consultation with school officials can resolve the issue before it becomes a problem. Some schools, with advance notice, will allow parents to visit the cafeteria and eat lunch. Be prepared to pay for your lunch.

Food for All

Breakfast must be available in all schools where it is needed. Schools must provide meals free or at reduced cost to those students whose families can't afford them.

Lunches From Home

There are no rules against letting a child bring lunch to school. One should remember, however, there probably won't be any place to secure it, so it should be packed in your child's backpack. It is very unlikely there will be any way to refrigerate it. Send food that won't spoil for lack of refrigeration and drinks in a Thermos or disposable container.

School-meal Costs

The price of a meal at a school cafeteria ranges from about $1 to $2.25, plus the cost of any a la carte items.

Most schools sell debit cards for the cafeteria. It's the parents' duty to load the card with money. It's the students' duty to spend down the card.

School cafeterias receive state and federal subsidies. Low-income students are entitled to reduced-cost or free meals. Check with your school principal. The program is confidential.

Lunch Schedule-Monitoring

Grades 1-5 or 1-6 line up outside their classes, walk over as a group, and are seated with their class. Adults, not necessarily the teachers, supervise the kids while they eat. Once finished, they are allowed to leave on their own and play until the bell sounds (practices may vary by district.)

Middle and junior-high and high-school students walk to the cafeteria on their own. Many high schools will have an outdoor eating area with tables or benches.

Some high schools allow their students to go off campus where they eat at a sandwich shop or cafe.

Smokers have to go off campus (two blocks) to light up. Some sneak off to the parking lot.

Many schools will have a staff member patrol the campus or the school neighborhood, often in a golf cart, during lunch hour.

Lunch period at many schools starts at 11:30 a.m.

Food Allergies And Special Diets

If your child has a special dietary need for medical or religious reasons, talk to your principal and cafeteria director. Provide any dietary guidelines ordered by your pediatrician, minister or rabbi. The same advice applies if your child is a vegetarian. Although some schools are equipped with special devices to treat allergic reactions, many aren't or too few people are trained in their use. Prevention is the best remedy.

Health And Schools

Beyond healthy meals, your child's school is obliged to safe-guard the health of all its students by requiring immunizations and establishing fitness standards through physical-education classes

Children infected with contagious or infectious diseases may be barred from enrolling. Parents must be notified when a child is barred for health reasons. A student living where a family member has a contagious disease may be barred from school if officials believe this poses a risk to other students.

Immunizations And Physical Exams

Before being admitted to a California public school, all children must be immunized against certain diseases. See Chapter 1, Enrollment, for the list of immunizations.

Don't take this list as the final word. Check with the school. Some counties might add a tuberculosis test. And often one immunization is not enough; some require booster shots.

Parents can request an exemption on moral or religious grounds or if they feel they are unsafe. The health exam can be waived if parents object or are unable for any reason to get a checkup for their child.

Parents using safety issues as a reason for exemption must present a doctor's statement that the proposed immunizations would be unsafe for their child.

Sick Or Hurt

California schools are not required to have school nurses. Most don't. If your district has a school nurse, ask if this person is a licensed nurse or a staff member. Ask also if the nurse regularly visits every school or is on call. Get a copy of the district's policy regarding illness and medications.

All medicine, including nonprescription, may be administered by school officials if they have a written statement from the prescribing doctor detailing the dosage, frequency of dosage and a note from the parents granting permission.

Many schools draw a line between dispensing pills and, say, injecting insulin. Some schools require the parents to come to the school and give their child needed medication. Remember, school personnel are there to educate your child; outside of the nurse, they are not trained medical professionals.

Schools require parents to fill out an emergency notification card listing their home and work numbers and an alternate relative or responsible person your child can be released to. If a health problem arises, the school will call you and ask you to come take your child home.

Inform officials of any chronic medical issues your child has and the need for medication.

Notify your child's school if you intend to be out of town and leave a name and telephone number of someone who can be responsible for your child if she gets sick while you are away. Also leave that person a copy of your child's health card and permission to seek medical attention.

Health Insurance

Students are not required to have health insurance. The only exceptions are student athletes who must have either their own plan or a district-offered plan. If you want health insurance for your children, schools and other groups have come up with a low-cost plan (See Chapter 1.)

Pregnant Students

As long as there is no medical reason to stay home, the girl must attend school. It's the law, married or not. School officials, however, can remove the student from the classroom if her pregnancy disrupts the education of the other students.

Many districts offer classes for married or pregnant teens, focusing on parent education, child development, prenatal care, job training and visits from a public health nurse. Ask your district what options are offered.

Pesticides

At the beginning of the school year, parents and school workers must be notified about pesticides expected to be used at the school. This notification will include an Internet address (www.schoolipm.info) that provides details about pesticides and their potential risks.

When a school knows it is going to zap bugs or weeds chemically, it must post a notice of intent 24 hours in advance, listing the chemicals to be used. This notice must remain up until at least 72 hours after the actual zapping.

Police And Security

In the wake of the Columbine and other school shootings, California districts are responding to the pressure for more security. It takes more than a fence to keep a school safe.

School districts may establish their own security team or police force. These officers lack the powers of regular police officers, although their chief must have had prior peace officer experience.

Many school districts work closely with the local police and some police departments assign officers to the high-school campuses. They enforce the laws, try to make the campus safer and often make friends with the students and steer them away from trouble.

Some high schools informally designate an administrator as an enforcer, someone who is good at projecting authority, spotting trouble and dealing with it. This person will be found walking around campus and being visible at football and basketball games and other school events.

Although schools worry about gang violence and crack down on gang colors, gangs are not a problem for many campuses. Many communities don't have gangs and when they do, "Your hard-core gang members aren't going to school," explained one police chief.

Many police departments run a DARE program (Drug Abuse and Resistance Education) program and assign an officer to visit schools regularly and steer the kids away from drugs. In the beginning, great hopes were pinned on DARE but critics are calling it useless.

Some schools are equipped with metal detectors to detect anyone bringing in weapons. Possessing weapons is a surefire way to get expelled, even if your kid brings them for self-protection.

Schools take other precautions. (See Chapter 14, Conduct and Consequences.)

Don't Gripe Or You're In Charge

One elementary school responded to students' complaints about food by letting them plan the menus for several months. After hearing the students' complaints, the cafeteria director and principal agreed to consult the pupils about their desires. The students were given a tour of the cafeteria and shown how things worked.

Their choices for the menu had to be based on budget, state nutrition standards and not a little common sense. The kids dove in, planned menus with the help of cafeteria staff and succeeded in producing more appealing (to other students) fare.

Crossing Guards

Fielded either by the city or the school district, crossing guards escort children and, sometimes, other pedestrians, through school crossings during the before and after school hours. They are trained, usually outfitted in an orange vest and equipped with a hand-held stop sign.

Motorists must stop when crossing guards enter an intersection with their signs, regardless if any children are present. Crossing guards earn about $12 to $14 per hour. Some communities have volunteer guards.

Dangerous Schools

If a school is deemed to be "persistently dangerous," students may transfer to another school or district, per federal regulations. The threshold for that label is based on the number of expulsions for serious offenses involving violence, weapons or drugs per 100 students for three consecutive years.

No California school has met that threshold and some people argue that the threshold is so high or so vague that it is unlikely ever to be exceeded.

Fire Drills and Earthquakes

In all schools, including the private ones, fire drills are mandatory. They must be held at least once a month in the elementary grades, four times during the school year in middle schools and twice a year in high schools.

All schools with 50 or more students or more than one classroom must have fire alarms.

As of 2002, any new school built in California must be equipped with alarms, smoke detectors and automatic sprinklers approved by the state fire marshal. Older schools have fire alarms but may not have smoke detectors or sprinklers. Any school proposing to spend $200,000 or more on upgrades must install smoke detectors and sprinklers. The fire alarms must be tested at least once every month.

Certain portable classrooms are exempt from these requirements.

When Mother Earth throws a hissy fit in California, it usually comes as an earthquake.

Periodic "drop and cover" drills in the schools and emergency preparedness kits assembled by parents and left at the schools are just some of the things districts do to prepare for temblors. Staff is trained in evacuation procedures. Your local district has a plan available for review.

California has tough building rules for schools because of the earthquakes. In the 1930s, an earthquake leveled school buildings in Long Beach, and really got people thinking. Since then, the state has been tightening school building codes. Every time we have a major earthquake, the experts examine what survived and what didn't and the codes are toughened accordingly. Buildings are torn down and replaced with seismically safe structures. Others may be allowed to remain standing but their seismic resistance is improved. We're still learning.

Earthquakes are not a matter of "if." They are a matter of

Earthquake Kit

- Use a one-gallon plastic bag (self-closing, zipper type). When it is filled, seal with heavy tape (like duct tape); mark your child's name and room number on the outside.
- Emergency form (student's name, etc.) Put form inside kit.
- Foil blanket. This blanket folds into a small packet and is designed to keep the kids warm.
- Small water (16 oz. plastic bottle) or 2-3 small cartons of juice (check date to ensure it will last the school year). Don't use glass containers.
- 2 plastic spoons
- 2 or 3 small flip-top type cans of fruit
- Brief letter to your child to offer reassurance
- Other suggestions (if space allows): 1 non-bulky T-shirt (for extra warmth), life savers, fruit roll-ups, energy bar, unsalted nuts, small pad of paper and pen for games, deck of cards, picture of your family, package of Kleenex tissues.
- If you don't want to make your own kit, you can buy one. Prices start about $20. Look in the yellow pages under Earthquake Products and Services.

"when." California is riddled with active faults.

For your peace of mind, tell your kids to call when a major earthquake strikes.

For information about how to prepare your home for earthquake, read the beginning of the phone book.

Unkempt Bathrooms

School bathrooms must be kept clean and equipped with toilet paper, soap, paper towels and other necessities or risk losing state funds. So says a law that took effect in 2004. School officials agree but say they still need the cooperation of students.

Comprehensive Safety Plans

All schools must have a safety plan covering issues from crime to natural disaster. Local plans must address:

- Assessing crime on campus and at school-related activities
- Procedures for reporting child abuse
- Disaster procedures
- Unsafe conduct that could result in disciplinary action
- Alerting teachers of dangerous pupils
- Discrimination and harassment polices
- Dress code ban on "gang-related apparel"
- Procedures to lets students and staff safely enter and leave campus
- Maintaining a safe and orderly learning environment
- Forbidding hate crimes

Physical Education

By law, California schools are required to offer:

- 200 minutes of physical education every ten days for grades 1 to 6 annually. This breaks out to about two hours a week.
- 400 minutes every 10 days for grades 7-8 or about 40 minutes a day annually. This requirement also applies to high-school students for each year they take P.E. Only two years are required in high school for graduation.

For more on physical fitness, see Sports, Chapter 11.

Tips For Lunches From Home

Here are some tips for preparing sack lunches that nutritionists say will not only be healthy and appetizing but can teach your child proper nutrition habits:

- *Eat what you preach. If you advocate low-fat, high-fiber, let your kids see you eating it at home, at least once in a while.*
- *Use buzz words such as "muscle food" or "brain food" or "climb high food." Relate the foods' benefits to an activity they support, for example milk's calcium builds strong bones and teeth, so call milk "bone-growing food."*
- *Let your kids help you shop for groceries, give them some influence on what to buy.*
- *Use some imagination, like cookie cutters for sandwiches.*
- *Add fruit slices or wedges to your child's water and chill it in the freezer. On warm days, partly-frozen drinks are thawed but still cold at lunch time.*
- *Offer variety and abundance, but keep it bite-sized.*
- *Pack in snacks such as raisins or cookies sweetened with real fruit juice.*

Lunchroom Conduct

Although the following were established by one school district, they can be applied to any elementary school:

- *Be quiet and orderly in the lunch line and at the tables.*
- *Follow the instructions of supervisors.*
- *Practice good table manners.*
- *Sit properly with legs and feet under the table.*
- *Never throw food or other objects.*
- *Pick up all trash at your seat and around your table.*
- *When you finish eating, raise your hand, remain seated and wait to be dismissed by a supervisor or teacher.*
- *Put all trash in lunch area trash cans.*

14

Conduct & Consequences

- **EXPECTATIONS OF STUDENTS**
- **DRESS CODES AND HAIR**
- **TOYS AND PARTIES**
- **OPEN OR CLOSED CAMPUS**
- **DETENTION, EXPULSION AND SUSPENSION**
- **ABSENT OR TARDY**
- **CURSING**
- **CARS AND PARKING**

Many teachers say the chief obstacle to learning is student conduct. Unruly, disrespectful students waste their time at the expense of students wanting to learn. Inexperienced teachers can be sitting ducks for a group of middle-schoolers bent on mischief.

Educators blame what they see as the decline of the family for much of the unruliness. Classroom control is as important an ingredient in teacher training as what and how to teach.

When students misbehave, there are consequences ranging from warnings to expulsion.

Students are subject to conduct codes when they are on school grounds, coming to or from school, during lunch whether on or off campus and while coming to or from or participating in a school-sponsored activity.

Policies vary among districts and schools but the issues addressed in this chapter pertain to all California public schools. Most districts provide a parents' handbook spelling out students' and parents' responsibilities regarding conduct.

Students' Responsibilities

Be on time, come to class every day and be prepared with pencils, paper and books when you get there.

A good night's sleep and a willingness to get along with your classmates and teachers are equally important.

Classroom Control

Classroom control is a term you'll hear a lot in the context of teachers. It refers to the teacher's control of the class or an old-fashioned word "discipline." Teachers who maintain order keep minor incidents from escalating into major ones and spend more time teaching.

Often the teacher will send a more unruly student to the principal's office. In some schools, it is common to see a line of students, and their parents, parked outside the principal's office waiting to be called.

In the larger schools, vice-principals assume this burden, counseling students and parents about everything from grabbing someone's cap, an offensive remark, a "mean" look or rough horseplay.

Attendance

State law says your child must attend school every day unless she's sick or there is a death in the immediate family. It's your responsibility to get her there on time every day. If she's more than 30 minutes late on three separate occasions or is absent without an excuse more than three times, she's a truant.

Then she risks suspension, getting poor grades or losing her driving privileges. You run the risk of jail. In 1999, a San Jose mom spent 50 days in jail after her three kids were absent almost a quarter of the school year. School officials contact parents by mail or telephone when their children are truants.

Another reason schools frown on unexcused absences: They lose about $30 per day for each pupil who is absent without a legitimate excuse. One cash-strapped superintendent in said in a letter that cutting unexcused absences by half would give the district an extra $500,000. Another district cracked down in 2003 when an audit showed truancy was costing it millions annually.

A student can be referred to a hearing before the Student Attendance Review Board if she has a history of poor attendance or disruptive behavior. In addition to school personnel, this board may include representatives of the police, district attorney, probation and health departments. After any hearing, the board can make a recommendation to transfer the student to another school or to an alternative education program.

Sickness

Every school has a procedure for parents to report when their children are sick. Usually a telephone number is provided for parents to call and report that Tommy is sick. Often parents are asked to give their child's name, grade, why he is absent and who is calling. If his absence is prolonged, you might be asked to provide a doctor's note saying that he can return to class.

Students must be given time to make up work missed because of excused absences. The amount of time, however, varies with the teacher.

Mr., Mrs., Ms. Or Teacher's First Name.

Many educators recommend Mr. or Ms. Using a teacher's first name undermines respect. Teachers probably would take the student aside privately and impress this on him, one veteran administrator says.

Gum In Class

Forget the old rule of bringing enough gum for everyone in class. If a student is caught chewing gum, she could be made to clean it off her desk and elsewhere in the school. Gum sticks on books, clothes, hair and shoes. Leave the gum at home or in the garbage before coming to class.

Interestingly, however, there are some studies that show some students concentrate better if they are chewing gum.

Hats And Caps

Most schools forbid wearing caps or hats inside. If the cap would stay on its owner's head, all would be fine. But caps frequently are snatched away and tossed around the classroom in a rowdy and disruptive game of "keep-away." Hooded jackets are OK so long as the hoods are down. Hoods over the head in class means a student is blocking the teacher out.

If your child has a medical reason for wearing the cap or hood indoors, get a doctor's note. Exceptions are made for religious requirements.

Dress Codes

Every district has a dress code. Safety, decency, self-respect and campus harmony are among the reasons.

Dress codes are sometimes controversial. Teachers and administrators want them, students think they're too rigid. Many schools sidestep the issue by requiring uniforms. Those uniforms vary widely, although they usually have in common slacks, skirts and collared shirts.

Read your district's code, then see how well it is being enforced. Although bans on bare-midriff clothing, flip-flop sandals, body piercing, inappropriate clothing logos and many others are on the books in various districts, enforcement may be spotty.

Says one administrator, "It's not the clothing, but does it get in the way of the educational process. It's quality versus quantity."

Wearing the wrong colors can be fatal in some schools, a circumstance that has prompted officials to ban the wearing of certain "gang" attire and colors. A Northern California youth was beaten to death because he was wearing what his assailants perceived to be the colors of a rival gang. They were mistaken, but that didn't protect the victim.

Another district barred students from wearing popular plastic bracelets after learning that the various colors signaled the wearers' sexual conduct.

Often the rule is: no problem, no ban. For example, a ban was imposed on clothing and skateboards bearing specific logos at one high school after the logos spurred racial tensions on campus. At another campus, the Oakland Raiders' logo was unwelcome because of its popularity with gang members.

Hair And Makeup

If your son's fancy is a star-spangled Mohawk hairdo, it may not be the school's fancy. In that case you have two choices, fight the school or fight your son.

State law doesn't specify when a hairdo becomes a hair-don't. It does, however, give administrators wide latitude by prohibiting anything that is "disruptive" or interferes with instruction. Wearing the school mascot on his shirt won't alienate your son from his teachers, but emblazoning it on his cranium probably will.

If your kid looks like Gene Simmons of KISS or Christina Aguilera's video "costume," that's too much. Best rule of thumb: If you the parent think it's too much, it is. Your kid's teacher will tell you if it's still too much.

Swearing

A minor slip won't get him expelled or suspended, at least not right away. Continued use of profanity and obscenities might.

Probably his teacher will tell him that swearing or cursing is not acceptable and that continued outbursts could send him to the principal's office for a meeting with Mom and Dad

"Even if it's a slip, we want to make sure it doesn't become habitual," one principal says.

Forgotten Homework

Everyone, kid or grown-up, forgets an assignment sometime. And while educators say they are teaching children to be responsible for their own assignments, every school has an office where parents can drop off forgotten lunches, homework, raincoats or lunch money.

Forget faxing or e-mailing your kid's homework to the school. Often the drop-off office isn't close enough to the fax machine and the staff member has other duties, leaving little time to check e-mail or faxes for every student who forgot an assignment.

Bottom line: Teach your kid responsibility or be prepared to drive in the lunches and assignments.

Dances And Grad Nite

How should kids behave at school dances and proms?

Boys, like gentlemen. Girls, like ladies.

Have fun. No fights, weapons, drugs or booze.

The same expectations prevail at Grad Nite, which is run by parents. Grad Nite participants are given a code of conduct or contract in advance. Read it and discuss it with your kids so they understand the rules and won't spoil anybody's fun.

Buses

Your daughter will be expected on either the school bus or public transit to remain seated during her ride and to refrain from eating or drinking. No gum, either. Other passengers don't like wearing it on their shoes or clothes.

Security cameras have been mounted on many school buses and public transit to prevent rowdiness and vandalism.

For more about buses, see Chapter 12, Schedules and Holidays.

CD Players And Toys

Most districts try to discourage students from bringing personal belongings such as skateboards, portable CD players or toys to school. They get lost, stolen or broken. Teachers don't want to deal with students grieving over their lost possessions or mediate ownership disputes.

That said, however, many districts permit CD players and even skateboards, making students responsible for any personal property they bring to school.

Cars And Parking

Welcome to the grown-ups' world. You've got a license and a car. Now try and find a parking place. Or so goes the response of many administrators stuck with too many student drivers and too few parking places.

At some schools, student parking is assigned by lottery. Others by grade scores, grade level and even others by who signs up first. Students are expected to obey all the rules of the road they learned to get their license.

Vandalism and theft are problems. Complaints from neighbors about parked cars are common, say administrators who admit they can't control off-campus parking.

A note to parents about your cars: Check with your school about drop-off and pick-up policies. Many control the direction of entrance and exit for parents picking up their children or dropping them off at school. The intent is an orderly flow of traffic and student safety. Remember the scene in the movie "Mr. Mom," where Michael Keaton got chewed out for not knowing the drop-off and pick-up routine? Well, for many schools it is an issue. Learn it early and save yourself some grief and embarrassment.

Parties

Thinking of celebrating your daughter's eighth birthday in the classroom with her teacher and classmates?

Check with her teacher first on both the party and the invitations. Party policies vary by grade and by school. Some districts will set aside the last 10-15 minutes of a day to observe a birthday. Others suggest such alternatives as donating a book in celebrating your child's birthday. One district's approach is to schedule two classroom parties annually: one before winter break and the other an end of the year party.

Invitations are often discouraged unless everyone in the class is invited.

Open And Closed Campus

An "open" campus is one where students may leave the school grounds at lunch, returning in time for their next class. A "closed" campus means the students must remain on campus until the end of the school day.

Sometimes this is a safety issue aimed at preventing fights, drug dealing or other illegal conduct. Sometimes it's a response to merchants' complaints about rowdy students disrupting their business.

Detention

A teacher may require a student who breaks a minor rule to remain after school. Typically, the student will work on her homework during that time, up to an hour. Before the student serves her detention, her parents are notified.

Every teacher has the discretion to impose some form of discipline to maintain order and reinforce the rules.

Suspension And Expulsion

Suspension and expulsion are punishment for serious offenses.

If your child is suspended, he will be out of school for up to five consecutive days or 20 days in a school year before he can come back. His teacher decides whether he will be allowed to make up any tests or assignments he missed.

An expulsion means he's out until the local school board agrees to let him back in.

If your son has been expelled, he can't go hang out at the mall or stay home and chill. State law requires that he continue his education. All districts have schools to continue the education of expelled students. Usually these are the community day school or county community schools established for expelled youths or those in juvenile hall or being supervised by the court.

The district's board of trustees has the authority to expel any student at the recommendation of school officials. If a student is recommended for expulsion, he is entitled to a hearing before the board. After being expelled, a student must petition the board before being readmitted to his old school. Even then, the board and school administrators can veto any return.

Students who are suspended or expelled are not in school, meaning they are not learning and the school is losing money based on attendance. One Southern California district reduced its suspensions significantly after implementing a series of intervention measures including teaching students more about the various ethnic groups on their campuses and employing on-campus suspensions where students remained at the school but out of the classroom's social environment.

Appeals

Expulsion orders can be appealed to the local school board and then on up to the county superintendent of schools.

Offenses

Actions by students that can result in expulsion or suspension usually involve criminal activity or acts of violence or harassment.

Since the shootings at Columbine High and other schools, officials aren't lightly dismissing threats. A middle-school student in an affluent district was suspended for two weeks because of what she left on her teacher's desk— a list entitled "People to die," and naming several students and the teacher. An 11-year-old was arrested after making threats in a school essay.

While the accused dismissed their actions as pranks, some of those on their lists were afraid to continue at the same school, officials said.

Students can be expelled or suspended for assault, sexual assault or harassment, fighting, misuse of school computers or e-mail, possessing or using a dangerous weapon, possessing or using tobacco products, cheating or stealing, frequent truancy, making terrorist threats, willfully defying school authorities and possessing, using or selling illegal drugs or alcohol.

Students accused of crimes involving drugs or violence or making terrorist threats are turned over to police.

Harassment

Sexual harassment is not condoned and students are suspended. Harassment includes bullying, intimidating, making disparaging or hurtful remarks towards someone because of their gender or sexual orientation. Students and school employees are covered by the policy.

School officials must act on all complaints of harassment.

Alternatives

By law, a student may be suspended or expelled only when all other means of correction fail or the student's continued presence on campus poses a threat to the safety of others. Other means of correction include detention, counseling, conflict management, meetings with the family or community service.

Some districts have what they call Saturday school, two hours perhaps of academics, two hours of picking up litter. (See Chapter 12, Schedule.)

Lockers

Lockers are school district property, not the student's. Police can't search lockers without a warrant or probable cause (such as seeing a student putting drugs or weapons in a locker) but school officials can. Many districts routinely search lockers and desks for weapons and drugs, sometimes with the aid of dogs. Many districts have removed their lockers.

Cheating

Submitting someone else's work as your own— be it written by a friend, relative or from a Web site —is plagiarism and cheating. School officials consider it the same as looking at someone else's answers during a test.

The school will discipline students caught cheating. That can range from a failing grade for the paper or assignment to suspension or even expulsion. Rarely will a school allow a student to make up such an assignment.

Smoking

Smoke if you got 'em, but not until you're 18 and at least two blocks off campus.

By law, nobody in California under the age of 18 is allowed to smoke. The same law bans smoking on campus by all adults and students. School officials are directed to "take all steps practical to discourage high-school students from smoking."

Cell Phones

Cellular phones and pagers, once equated with drug deals, are permitted on campus now — with certain restrictions. Use during class is considered disruptive. Teachers have the authority to ban them from the classroom. Advise your child to set her phone on silent page and return the call after class.

Vandalism

The law says that you are liable for up to $10,000 if your child's misconduct caused death, injury or damage to school property or a school employee's personal property. His grades and diploma can be held up until the claim is paid. On top of that your kid can go to jail or even state prison, depending on the severity of the damage and his age.

If you are unable to pay the damages, your son can be put to work until the claim is satisfied.

Free Speech

Students have the right of free speech. If your child wishes to disagree respectfully, she should have no fear of retaliation.

State law grants students the same free speech rights as adults.

Student journalists are responsible for their actions, the same as adult journalists. A faculty adviser is responsible for seeing that the students maintain professional standards and for protecting the school's liability.

The students' free speech actions must not disrupt the educational process or incite unlawful acts. Obscenity and libel laws do apply to students, the same as they do to adults.

For example, 50 high-school students were suspended for participating in an antiwar protest. While peace activists called the suspensions unfair, school officials said they had warned the students in advance not to walk out of class to join the protest.

Alameda County school officials in 1990 successfully defended a student newspaper sued by a teacher for negative comments about him. An appeals court ruled they were subjective remarks and could not be proved as true or false. Students have free speech but they can be sued and, in some cases, punished by school authorities if they are irresponsible.

Lost And Found

Handling lost items varies from school to school. Usually lost items are taken to a central location where they can be reclaimed. It is helpful to have your children's names written somewhere on their clothes and personal items. Find out how lost-and-found works at your school. Caution is advised, however. Some teachers have warned their pupils they will toss forgotten items into the trash if left overnight.

15

Private Schools & Tutors

Three Questions

For perhaps discomforting reasons, finding a private school for your child is fairly easy — you don't have too many choices.

Once you have answered three screening questions, you will often narrow your choices to three or four schools or fewer.

- **Religious or secular?** The majority of private schools in the state are affiliated with a religion or to a much lesser extent, an ethnic group, notably Jewish, French or Armenian.

  The Catholic Church, by far, runs the biggest system of private education in the state. Religious schools accept nonmembers but give preference to families that actively practice the religion. Incidentally, religious schools are often called parochial schools; secular schools, independents.

- **How much tuition can you afford?** If the answer is $11,000-$12,000 or more, the choices will leap off the page; they are that few. These schools are found in coastal counties or the San Francisco Bay Area usually in or near affluent communities.

  Although the schools offer scholarships and financial aid, they need families who can afford the tuition.

  If you're looking in the $3,000 to $6,000 range for elementary schools, your choices increase.

- **Immediate neighborhood?** Or long drive or boarding school (California does have a few.)?

  If immediate neighborhood, your local phone directory might be all that you need. In its relocation guides, McCormack's publishes private school directories for the metropolitan counties. These guides list the larger schools by city and give their enrollment, addresses and phone numbers. See end of book or go to www.mccormacks.com.

Fingertip Facts

• California enrolls about 609,483 students in private schools, about 9 percent of all students in the state.

• Of these, 34% or 208,000 students attend schools in Los Angeles County.

• Of the remaining, 249,000 or about 41% percent of all private-school students will be found in Alameda, Contra Costa, Santa Clara, San Mateo, San Francisco, Orange, San Diego and Sacramento counties.

• Which is to say that nine counties account for about 75 percent of all private-school students in the state.

• San Francisco leads the state in percent of students attending private schools — 30 percent. Many parents dislike the public school system, which transfers many children out of their neighborhoods. San Francisco has a long tradition of private schools and neighborhood Catholic schools.

• In 2003, California counted 2,700 schools that enrolled 30 or more students. Of these, schools affiliated with a religion tallied about 1,850 or 69 percent of the total.

• Catholic schools number about 700. Almost all of them have enrollments of at least 200. The high schools range in enrollments from about 400 to 1,200, with perhaps one or two a little higher.

• Other religious schools include, Christian (very popular in some counties; large enrollments), Baptist, Seventh Day Adventists, Assembly of God, Lutheran, Pentacostal, Episcopalian, Jewish.

• Many independent schools are organized around a specific teaching philosophy. The most popular appear to be: Montessori, Carden and Walden (described later in this chapter.)

• Many schools are mom and pop operations, literally. For legal reasons, the family forms itself into a "school" and mom and dad educate the kids at home. A support network has sprung up to help these schools.

• Charter schools are not private schools; they are governed in some way by the state of California or a local school district. Unions distrust charters and when the legislation was written, it prohibited any existing private school from turning itself into a charter. Many arguments over this. Religious schools cannot be charter schools or receive public funding, another sore point.

Private Schools — the Downside

Although private schools often enjoy a better reputation than public, they are not without their problems. The typical private or parochial school is funded way below its public-school counterpart.

In size, facilities and playing fields and in programs, public schools usually far outstrip private schools. Private-school teachers earn less than public school teachers. "Typical" has to be emphasized. The high-tuition schools often are not typical.

High-tuition Schools

These schools are generally well-equipped, pay their teachers competitively and limit many classes to fewer than 17 students.

They offer an advanced curriculum (a sixth-grade student might be working at a seventh- or eighth-grade level), full-time teachers in art, music and foreign languages, field trips to supplement classroom curriculum and intramural sports.

These schools frequently test applicants for their learning and social skills. Some, seeking social and ethnic diversity, offer scholarships or financial aid to low- or moderate-income families.

But Even When Typical ...

Private schools enjoy certain advantages over public schools.

Public schools must accept all students, have almost no power to dismiss the tenured incompetent and are at the mercy of their neighborhoods for the quality of students. The unruly often cannot be expelled or effectively disciplined.

Much has been said about the ability of private schools to rid themselves of problem children and screen them out in the first place. But tuition, even when modest, probably does more than anything else to assure private schools quality students.

Parents who pay extra for their child's education and often agree to work closely with the school are, usually, demanding parents. The result: fewer discipline problems, fewer distractions in the class, more of a willingness to learn.

When you place your child in a good private school, you are, to a large extent, buying him or her scholastic classmates. They may not be the smartest children — many private schools accept children of varying ability — but generally they will have someone at home breathing down their necks to succeed in academics.

The same attitude, a reflection of family values, is found in the high-achieving public schools. When a child in one of these schools or a private school turns to his left and right, he will see and later talk to children who read books and newspapers. A child in a low-achieving school, public or private, will talk to classmates who watch a lot of television and rarely read.

These are, necessarily, broad generalizations. Much depends on whom the children pick for friends. High-achieving students certainly watch television but, studies show, much less than low-achieving students. Many critics contend that even high-scoring schools are graduating students poorly prepared for college.

The Quality Of Teaching

Do private schools have better teachers than public schools? Impossible to tell. Both sectors sing the praises of their teachers.

Private schools, compared to public, have much more freedom to dismiss teachers but this can be abused. The private schools themselves advise parents to avoid schools with excessive teacher turnover.

Although most can't pay as much as public schools, private institutions claim to attract people fed up with the limitations of public schools, particularly the restrictions on disciplining and ejecting unruly children. Some proponents argue that private schools attract teachers "who really want to teach."

The Political Argument

This is something that is rarely discussed on TV or in newspapers but shows up in academic journals, books and political magazines. Many conservatives argue that the public schools are fatally flawed, that because of union and civil service rules they are unable to solve problems, no matter how well they are funded. Many of these arguments point to urban schools that year in and out post low scores. The proponents do not say private schools will perform miracles. They argue that private schools, being more flexible and more in control of their staffs, are able to do a better job for less money. The unions disagree and advance their own arguments, usually calling for more money for public schools and more training for teachers.

Religion And Private Schools

Some private schools are as secular as any public institution. But many are religion-oriented and talk in depth about religion or ethics, or teach a specific creed. Or possibly they teach values within a framework of western civilization or some other philosophy.

Public schools teach the history of major religions and touch on the basic tenets of each, and try to inculcate in the children a respect for all religions. It's hard, if not impossible, however, for public schools to talk about values within a framework of religion or a system of ethics. Often, it's difficult for them to talk about values. Some people argue that this is a major failing.

Many religious schools accept students of different religions or no religion. Some schools offer these students broad courses in religion — less dogma. Ask about the program.

Teaching Philosophies

Among the private schools, several teaching philosophies stand out. Only schools that subscribe to these philosophies and the teaching methods prescribed are allowed to incorporate the names such as Carden, Montessori and Waldorf.

Carden Schools: Mae Carden opened her School for Young Children in New York in 1934. Her students' achievements impressed others who persuaded her to share her teaching philosophy and methods. Formal education in the Carden approach starts with three-year-olds and continues building on that foundation each year. Carden schools, to quote one Carden publication, "emphasize the fundamentals of how to study, organize materials, listen, think and reason ... and teach children to read with understanding and attain strong foundations in English, mathematics and science."

Montessori Schools: Montessori emphasizes active learning, one where the students go beyond sitting and "passively" learning through "mindless memorization." Students are encouraged to read material that hasn't been assigned and ask questions and think for themselves. The curriculum is integrated. For example, a study of Africa includes reading about African folklore, creating masks and block print dashikis in art, learning traditional African songs and study the continent's varied ecosystems.

Waldorf Schools: Waldorf schools were influenced by the defeat of Germany in World War I. Austrian scientist Rudolf Steiner developed the Waldorf method demanding that the children be free of economic or political influences. The Waldorf method contends children relate what they learn to their own experience. In early childhood children play at cooking, dressing up like their parents and become parents, rulers, all the while singing, painting and playing. Through this they develop a lifelong love of learning. The succeeding levels of childhood, middle and adolescence, repeat this exploration of the world in more sophisticated models.

Many independent schools might embrace some of these concepts. Others, such as French-American or Armenian-American, incorporate a specific international curriculum that also satisfies the California standards.

Money

Private-school parents pay taxes for public schools and they pay tuition. Public-school parents pay taxes but not tuition. Big difference.

Many private schools offer financial aid and discounts for siblings. Parents take on some of the school's jobs and keep costs down. Day care is extra. Fees might be charged for books and supplies. Parents might have to purchase uniforms. There may be an application fee. Private schools generally do a good job of laying out the costs. They don't want misunderstandings.

Admissions Procedures

Procedures vary by school. Where the children start as kindergarten students, some of these steps will not apply. Religious schools are interested in academics and in meeting what they see as the spiritual needs of their community. If a child is struggling with academics and comes from a church family, the religious schools often will admit her or him.

- Report card from last school.
- Recommendation from last teacher.
- Completion of a standardized test.
- Child makes an extended classroom visit (up to a full day).
- Parents interview.
- Financial screening (this is not required by many schools).
- Admissions decision made by committee.

Choosing A Private School

1. Inspect the grounds, the school's buildings, ask plenty of questions. "I would make myself a real pest," advised one private school official. The good schools welcome this kind of attention.

2. Choose a school with a philosophy congenial to your own and your child's. See Montessori, Carden, etc.

3. Ask whether the school is accredited. Private schools are free to run almost any program they like, to set any standards they like, which may sound enticing but in some aspects might hurt the schools. A few bad ones spoil the reputation of the good.

Many private schools sign up for inspections by independent agencies, such as the Western Association of Schools and Colleges and the California Association of Independent Schools. These agencies try to make sure that schools meet their own goals. Some good schools do not seek accreditation.

4. Get all details about tuition carefully explained.

5. Progress reports. Parent conferences. How often are they scheduled?

6. What are the entrance requirements? When must they be met? Although many schools use entrance tests, they often are employed to place the child in an academic program, not exclude him from the school.

7. For prep schools, what percentage of the students go on to college and to what colleges?

8. How are discipline problems handled?

9. What are the teacher qualifications? What is the teacher turnover rate?

10. How sound financially is the school? How long has it been in existence? There is nothing wrong per se with new schools. But you want a school that has the wherewithal to do the job.

11. Do parents have to work at functions? Are they required to "volunteer"?

12. Don't choose in haste but don't wait until the last minute. Some schools fill quickly, some fill certain classes quickly. If you can, call the school the year before your child is to enter, early in the year.

13. Don't assume that because your child attends a private school you can expect everything will go all right, that neither the school nor the student needs your attention. The quality of private schools in California varies widely.

Homeschooling

Another alternative to public schools in California is homeschooling. There are several options:

- A public school-independent study program.
- A private school-independent study program.
- Filing an affidavit with the state declaring your home a private school.
- Teaching your child at home yourself or with a tutor.

California has no law regulating homeschools, state education officials acknowledge, nor are there any requirements that parents notify local school officials of their intentions.

However, a homeschooled child could be at risk of truancy charges if caught out and about during regular school hours. Local districts are required to enforce truancy laws. The subject of homeschooling is a sensitive one to state officials who say that an effort in 2002 toward some regulation was met with a major outcry from homeschool advocates.

The California Homeschool Network can provide advice and information about homeschooling at (800) 327-5339 or its Web site: www.californiahomeschool.net

Ethnic Diversity

Many private schools are integrated and the great majority of private-school principals — the editor knows no exceptions — welcome minorities. Some principals fret over tuition, believing that it keeps many poor students out of private schools. Money, or lack of it, weighs heavily on private schools. Scholarships, however, are awarded, adjustments made, family rates offered.

More Information

See McCormack's Guides for school directories for metropolitan counties.

In San Francisco Bay area, Pince-Nez Press publishes four books on Bay Area private schools. Go to: www.pince-nez.com.

See also, The Los Angeles Guide to Private Schools, Soho Press, (212) 260-1900.

Catholic Schools

The following is based on interviews with Catholic educators. Many schools of other denominations will have similar rules.

- **All races, creeds welcome.** But where schools are full, preference is given to Catholic children from families active in parish, and siblings. After that, to active Catholics unable to get into own parish schools.

  High schools recruit regionally for students. Admissions tests but many accept average students. Standards vary by school.

- **Why parents send kids to Catholic schools.** Results of survey: academics, discipline, religion, safety. Order changes by parish. What happens in public schools affects enrollment in Catholic schools, said one educator.

  "Parents are looking for a safe, positive environment," said another.

- **Curriculum.** Elementary schools cover same basic subjects as public schools but weave in religious-moral viewpoint. "Philosophy based in Jesus Christ. Religious values are integral to learning experience." State textbooks often used. Each school picks texts.

  High school instruction, although varied, is greatly influenced by requirements of University of California.

  Educators advise parents to approach high schools as they would any educational institution: ask about grades, what percentage of students go on to college, whether school is accredited.

- **Non-Catholics.** Same instruction as Catholics, including history of Church and scripture. Attend Mass but not required to take sacraments. "We don't try to convert them," said one nun.

- **Corporal punishment.** Thing of past. Stress positive discipline, name on board, detention, probation.

- **Few expulsions.** Try to work with kid, parents to solve problems. Elementary expulsions usually have to be approved by diocese. Often parents withdraw child before he or she can be expelled.
- **Class sizes.** Maximum 35, minimum 25. A few higher and lower. Average about 30, somewhat smaller for high schools because of special classes, e.g., French. Would like smaller classes but point out that with well-behaved students, teachers can accomplish a lot. Matter of economics. If parents wanted smaller classes, they would have to pay more.

"We want to keep affordable prices so all people can choose us, not just rich."

- **Tuition.** Assistance often available.
- **Schedule.** Similar to public schools. 180 teaching days, 8:30 a.m. to 3 p.m.
- **Ability grouping.** In elementary grades (K-8) not done by class. Some grouping within classes, advanced children working at one level, slow children at another. Tutoring after class.

All high schools run prep programs, tend to attract prep students, but will accept remedial students if they have remedial instruction. Admission standards vary by high school.

Scores also vary by school — socioeconomics. Suburban Catholic schools tend to score higher than city schools.

- **Report cards.** At least four a year, plus results of state tests. Parents are expected to attend conferences, back-to-school nights.
- **Teacher quality.** Hired for competence and commitment to Catholic educational philosophy. No restriction in hiring non-Catholics but the system tends to attract Catholic teachers. "No trouble in attracting high-quality applicants."
- **Uniforms.** Yes, generally skirts, blouses for girls, collared shirts, trousers for boys. High schoolers have more sartorial discretion.

- **Extended care.** Many schools offer before- and afterschool care. Ask.

- **Drugs.** "We're not immune to dangers of the larger society," said one educator. Schools try to work with kids.

- **Extracurricular activities.** Although small, schools try to offer variety of activities, sports, arts, music. At elementary school, much depends on work of parents. "Parents are expected to do a lot."High schools offer good variety: music, band, arts, intramural sports, many club activities, cycling, golf.

Catholic high schools usually field very competitive football and basketball teams. "They help build school pride."

DeLa Salle High in Concord (in Northern California) may be the national football champ. It has not lost a game in decades. Another football power, Mater Dei in Santa Ana (Southern Cal).

For more information, call school directly.

Private Enrollments By County

County	All Students	All Schools	County Pop.
Alameda	28,414	172	1,496,200
Contra Costa	18,727	110	994,900
Santa Clara	36,735	176	1,729,900
San Mateo	16,407	78	717,000
San Francisco	25,458	112	791,600
Orange	56,561	310	2,978,800
San Diego	43,509	290	2,961,600
Los Angeles	208,268	1,206	9,979,600
Sacramento	22,911	151	1,309,600
Riverside	14,642	109	1,705,500
San Bernardino	21,848	195	1,833,000

Source: California Dept. of Education, 2004.

Kumon and Kaplan, etc.

Private firms have opened after-school centers throughout California. Among the most popular, Kumon, which has about 235 centers in the state. Kumon specializes in math and reading. See Kumon.com.

Kaplan offers instruction in a variety of subjects but is perhaps best known for its SAT tutoring. See Kaplan.com.

For other firms, see the phone directory under schools or tutoring.

Tutors

Many parents use them to get their kids over the rough spots or to make up the deficiencies of the school.

To find a tutor, usually the simplest way is to go the local phone directory and look under tutoring. Prices vary but in many instances the charges will run about $50 an hour.

If you are strapped for money, there are alternatives. Many retired teachers, for $35-50 an hour or lower, do a little tutoring on the side. They pass the word to the local teachers and the regulars, when queried by parents, say, you might call Mr. X or Ms. Y. The regulars often don't want to get involved in the tutoring; they don't want to give guarantees for the tutors or imply that the tutors can solve all problems.

Another alternative for the strapped: hire a high-school or community-college student who has something on the ball and can help the kids with homework or maybe basic math. This may not be the best solution but it might bring improvements.

Instead of one-to-one tutoring, you might try small groups, if you can find this arrangement.

The professional tutoring service will often test the students and work out a program. This is one advantage of this service but it can be costly.

Many schools have tutoring. You should check with the school to see what's available.

Index